Written by Rigoberto Garcia PhD
Enovation Press Corp 11

Accelerates SharePoint 2010 End User training course teaches students the basics of collaborating in SharePoint 2010 using Contacts, Tasks, Links, Calendar, and document libraries. Attendees also learn to use social networking capabilities such as blogs and wikis as well as how to customize SharePoint 2010 for improved efficiency and productivity.

Introduction to
SharePoint 2010
End Users (Edition)

11

ι

-

ABOUT THIS BOOK

In almost every office around the world, people communicate and share ideas to create products and services. This information sharing often requires the use of multiple software and web applications that do not necessarily work together perfectly. In contrast, Microsoft® SharePoint® Foundation combines familiar office tools, adds the latest technology, and extends the functionality of applications and the web into a single environment to share information and collaborate with colleagues, no matter where you are or how you access the information.
In this book, as a team site user, you will create and edit content in a Microsoft SharePoint
Foundation team site, and then you will also create and manage your own team site.

There was a time when individuals sat at a desk and worked on an entire project from start to finish with maybe just a few phone calls or a walk over to a coworker's desk to get some information. This approach will work for a project that involves only one or two individuals who are located in the same office, but will not be efficient for projects that require the efforts of numerous people and resources located in very diverse geographical locations. Using only email, desktop applications, and instant messaging to meet the information and communication needs of large teams and projects are cumbersome and time consuming. By implementing and using Microsoft SharePoint Foundation 2010, you can eliminate these disadvantages and leverage the power and flexibility of one of the most sophisticated software tools for team collaboration available today.

Since the class setup requirements for this book are very complex, simulations are provided for all the hands-on activities in the book. If you choose to, you can run the simulations provided to perform the activities in class or to review after class. A detailed description of the required setup is also provided for reference and for your use if you prefer to create a live environment for the class.

Course Description

Target Student

This book is designed for individuals who will need to access information on a Microsoft
SharePoint team site or for individuals who may need to create and manage a team site. This book is not intended for SP Farm Administrators.

Course Prerequisites

To ensure your success, we recommend that you first:

- ✓ Working Knowledge of browser functionality
- ✓ Knowledge of SharePoint technology
- ✓ Basic knowledge of Networking
- ✓ Basic knowledge of Windows 7 Operating Syste
- ✓ Basic Knowledge of Microsoft Office 2010 Suite of Applications
- ✓ Should be a PowerUser in their Job Description.
- ✓ Experience accessing information via a web browser.
- ✓ Basic Knowledge of Web Development Concepts

How to Use This Book

As a Learning Guide

This book is divided into lessons and topics, covering a subject or a set of related subjects. In most cases, lessons are arranged in order of increasing proficiency.

The results-oriented topics include relevant and supporting information you need to master the content. Each topic has various types of activities designed to enable you to practice the guidelines and procedures as well as to solidify your understanding of the informational material presented in the book.

- ✓ Create a team site.
- ✓ Perform basic site administration.

Course Requirements

Hardware

You will need two classroom servers and sufficient client computers for all students in the class, plus one client computer for the instructor. For each of these machines, the following hardware requirements are the minimum suggested for this book:

- ✓ 64-bit, four-core processor, 2.5 GHz minimum per core is required for installing the Windows Server 2008 R2 where Microsoft SharePoint Foundation 2010 will be installed.
- ✓ Duo or Quad Core Intel Processor 1 GHz CPU or higher for client systems.

- ✓ Minimum of 4 GB of RAM for each client computer or Higher.
- ✓ 16 GB RAM for single Windows 2008 R2 Server installation
- ✓ 80 GB of free hard disk space for installation of the Windows Server 2008 R2 fully Patched
- ✓ SQL Server 2008 R2.
- ✓ 40 GB or larger hard-disk drive for each student and instructor computer.
- ✓ DVD drive.
- ✓ VGA or higher video.
- ✓ Keyboard and mouse.
- ✓ You need to have an Internet connection because some of the software components are installed from the Internet.

Software

Domain Controller/Mail Server

The following software is required for the server that will function as the domain controller mail server.

- ✓ Windows Server 2008 R2 SP1 with Service Pack 2
- ✓ Internet Explorer 8.0 or 9.0

SharePoint Foundation 2010

The following software is required for installing SharePoint Foundation 2010.

- ✓ The 64-bit edition of Windows Server 2008 Enterprise with SP2. If you are running Windows

Server 2008 without SP2, the Microsoft SharePoint Products and Technologies 2010
Preparation Tool installs Windows Server 2008 SP2 automatically.

- ✓ SharePoint Foundation 2010
- ✓ Microsoft .NET Framework version 3.5 SP1
- ✓ Internet Explorer 8.0

At the back of the book, you will find a glossary of the definitions of the terms and concepts used throughout the book. You will also find an index to assist in locating information within the instructional components of the book.

As a Review Tool

Any method of instruction is only as effective as the time and effort you, the student, are willing to invest in it. In addition, some of the information that you learn in class may not be important to you immediately, but it may become important later. For this reason, we encourage you to spend some time reviewing the content of the book after your time in the classroom.

As a Reference

The organization and layout of this book make it an easy-to-use resource for future reference. Taking advantage of the glossary, index, and table of contents, you can use this book as a first source of definitions, background information, and summaries

.

Course Objectives

In this book, you will use, create, and edit content in a team site. You will also create and perform basic management of a team site using SharePoint Foundation 2010.
You will:

- ✓ identify basic functions of collaboration technology and Microsoft SharePoint Foundation
- ✓ 2010 team sites.
- ✓ add and modify list items and work with list views.
- ✓ add, edit, and share documents across libraries and wikis.
- ✓ communicate and collaborate with team members.
- ✓ work remotely with SharePoint content.
- ✓ customize your SharePoint environment.

Client Computers

The following software is required for the instructor computer and each student computer.

- ✓ Microsoft® Windows® 7 Enterprise or Ultimate Edition
- ✓ Microsoft .NET Framework 4.0, with Service Pack 1 installed
- ✓ Microsoft® Office® 2010 Professional or Professional Plus
- ✓ Microsoft Internet Explorer 9.0

a. Click **Site Actions**, **Site Settings**.

b. Under **Users and Permissions**, click **People and groups.**

c. In the **Quick Launch** bar, click **Team Site Owners.**

> d. On the **People And Groups: Team Site Owners** page, click **New.**
>
> e. Type *central*
>
> f. Click **OK.**
>
> g. Click **SSIC\Administrator, Sign Out,** and then click **Yes.**

Create and Share the Backup Folder

1. On the WSPF server, create a folder **Backup** and enable sharing for **Everyone.**

2. Give **Full Control** permission to **Everyone.**

Table of Content

Chapter 1

Introduction Microsoft® SharePoint® Foundation 2010

In this lesson, you will identify basic functions of collaboration technology and Microsoft SharePoint Foundation 2010 team sites. You will:

- ✓ Define the capabilities of Microsoft SharePoint Foundation 2010.

- ✓ ☐Identify the features of a Microsoft SharePoint Foundation team site.

Introduction

Microsoft SharePoint Foundation is an application that is built on top of Internet Information Services (IIS) and the Microsoft ASP.NET Framework. A set of servers that run the various components of SharePoint Foundation is called a server farm. A server farm can contain multiple front-end web servers and multiple Microsoft SQL Server database servers. Each farm has its own configuration database on the database server. The configuration database contains information about the front-end web servers in a farm and administrators of the farm. In SharePoint Foundation, all the content, including user information, is stored in a content database. Every server farm can have multiple content databases. For more information about SharePoint Foundation architecture, see Server and Site Architecture: Object Model Overview..

Sites based on SharePoint Foundation 2010, called SharePoint sites collection, take file storage to a new level, providing communities for team collaboration that make it possible for users to collaborate on documents, tasks, and events, and make it easier for them to share contacts and other information. SharePoint Foundation 2010 enables managers of teams and sites to manage site content and user activity easily.

Microsoft SharePoint Foundation 2010 is the essential solution for organizations that need a secure, manageable, Web-based collaboration platform. It helps teams stay connected and productive by providing easy access to the people, documents, and information that they need to make well-informed decisions and get work done.

In this book, you will create and edit content in a Microsoft SharePoint Foundation team site as well as create and manage your own team site. Before you can perform these tasks, you will need to understand the capabilities of collaboration software in general and Microsoft SharePoint Foundation in particular. In this lesson, you will identify basic functions of collaboration technology and Microsoft SharePoint Foundation 2010 team sites.

Lesson **1.1**

Microsoft SharePoint Foundation 2010

Before you can begin using Microsoft SharePoint Foundation 2010, you need to understand the technology and become familiar with the overall structure of a SharePoint site. In this topic, you will describe Microsoft SharePoint Foundation 2010.

Any new technology requires a learning curve when you encounter it for the first time. Initially, cell phones and PDAs were the cutting edge of technology. The applications and features these tools provided were fascinating but confusing. However, once cell phones and PDAs became common place, the mystery was gone and they became everyday tools just like the television or the radio. Microsoft SharePoint Foundation is a new technology that, at first glance, can seem very challenging. However, with some basic information, you can demystify the concepts and start working productively in the SharePoint environment.

Collaboration Technology

Definition: *Collaboration technology* is software that enables a group of individuals to achieve a common goal by facilitating information sharing and communication in one central location. Collaboration technology organizes and stores information for project teams or departments and makes the information available to team members located all over the world. Collaboration technology is generally web based and the information is accessible via company intranet or the Internet.

Microsoft SharePoint 2010 collaboration software provides enterprise-scale capabilities to meet business-critical needs such as managing content and business processes, simplifying how people find and share information across boundaries, and enabling informed decisions. Using the combined collaboration features of SharePoint 2010—which includes Microsoft SharePoint Foundation 2010 and Microsoft SharePoint Server 2010—plus the design and customization capabilities of Microsoft SharePoint Designer 2010, organizations can enable their users to create, manage, and easily build SharePoint sites that are discoverable throughout the organization.

Collaboration Technology vs. Standalone Applications

Today, commonly used collaboration tools include emails, wikis, instant messaging, video conferencing, blogs, and social networking sites. Individuals use email to communicate and share documents. In contrast, a word processing program is not considered collaboration technology. Although more than one person can modify a document, a word processing application does not create a collaborative environment because it does not provide the means to share information or communicate with other individuals.

Microsoft SharePoint Server & Foundation 2010

Microsoft SharePoint Foundation 2010 is a collaboration software product that enables individuals working on a project team or in a functional group to share information and communicate with one another from a central location. It allows users to work in a web-based collaborative environment. Microsoft SharePoint Foundation provides specialized sites that contain elements including a central calendar, task lists, libraries of documents, discussion boards and various other elements. Team members can access the site via a web browser from their PC or a PDA. SharePoint sites can be rendered offline to access information if an Internet connection is not available. SharePoint also integrates seamlessly with Microsoft Office applications in a single environment.

The Microsoft SharePoint Product Family

There are currently three products in the SharePoint family:

- ✓ Microsoft SharePoint Foundation 2010—the basic service for team site and subsite creation and administration.

- ✓ *Microsoft SharePoint Server 2010–* server application software that extends the functionality of Microsoft SharePoint Foundation 2010.

- ✓ Microsoft SharePoint Designer 2010 (SPD 2010)— web designer application software that is optimized for creating SharePoint sites.

The SharePoint Site Hierarchy

One of the most confusing subjects for me to grasp early on understood the SharePoint hierarchy. I couldn't tell a web application from a site collection. It confused me to no end. Well, after much study it seems rather simple now! Here's a diagram with a short explanation.

At the top of the hierarchy are server farms (SPFarms). This encompasses all the physical servers that comprise your SP installation. It may consist of single server install or multiple servers. SPFarms can share data amongst themselves or be self-serving. When you run the SP configuration wizard after installing MOSS/SPF you either create a new server farm or connect to an existing one. It's done once.

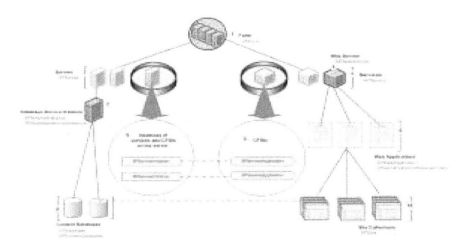

Once you have your server farm, the second layer of a SharePoint Server is the Services layer (SPServices), below that layer is the web application layer. This is what creates a corresponding website in IIS to host the site. This is where it gets its application pool and other IIS properties. You can create multiple web applications on a server farm. In SharePoint 2010 once the web application is install than the Site Collection or top level sites are deployed, this Site becomes the root, after that many subwebs can be deployed.

Now you have a hollow web application but nothing else. Enter site collections. It is simply a collection of SharePoint sites inside the web application. Here you define a top-level site. You can have multiple site collections.

SP Farm

Definition: The SPFarm object is the highest object within the SharePoint Foundation object model hierarchy. The Servers property gets a collection representing all the servers in the deployment, and the Services property gets a collection representing all the services.

The SPFarm object is the top node in the extensible configuration object model, which is designed to interact with the configuration data store. It contains global settings for all the servers, services, and solutions that are installed in a server farm. Use the Servers, Services, or Solutions property to retrieve these collections.

To access the current server farm object, you can use members on SPFarm.Local. For example, to return an SPServiceCollection object that represents the collection of services in the current server farm, use SPFarm.Local.Services. In addition, you can use the Farm property of classes that derive from the SPPersistedObject class, or you can use the Farm property of the SPSolution class, to get the server farm of the current object or solution

```
Dim farm As SPFarm = SPFarm.Local
Dim service As SPWebService =
farm.Services.GetValue < SPWebService > ""

Dim webApp As SPWebApplication

For Each webApp In  service.WebApplications
   Dim job As SPJobDefinition

   For Each job In  webApp.JobDefinitions

     If job.Name = "MyCustomJobDefinitionName"
Then
        j.Delete()
     End If
   Next job

   Dim newJob As New
MyCustomJobDefinition("MyCustomJobDefinition
Name", webApp)
   Dim schedule As SPSchedule =
SPSchedule.FromString("every 5 minutes between
0 and 59")
   newJob.Schedule = schedule

   newJob.Update()
Next webApp
```

Any public static (Shared in Visual Basic) members of this type are thread safe. Any instance members are not guaranteed to be thread safe.

SP Server

Definition: Each SPServer object represents a physical server computer. The ServiceInstances property provides access to the set of individual service instances that run on the individual computer.

Use either the Servers property of the SPFarm class, or the SPServerCollection constructor, to get the collection of servers that are used in the specified server farm. Use an indexer to return a single server from the collection. For example, if the collection is assigned to a variable named myServers, use myServers[index] in C#, or myServers(index) in Visual Basic, where index is either the GUID or the name that identifies the service.

```
SPServerCollection servers =
SPFarm.Local.Servers;
SPServer myServer =
servers["myExistingServer"];
myServer.Name = "NewServerName";
myServer.Role = SPServerRole.Application;
myServer.Update();
```

SP Service

Definition: Each SPService object represents a logical service installed in the server farm. Derived types of the SPService class include, for example, objects for Windows services, such as the timer service, search, the database service, etc. and also objects for Web services, such as the basic content publishing Web service which supports the Web applications.

SP WebService

Definition: An SPWebService object provides access to configuration settings for a specific logical service or application. The WebApplications property gets the collection of Web applications that run the service.

If the service implements the Service Application Framework of SharePoint Foundation, then it can be split into multiple configured farm-scoped instantiations (CFSIs). Each of these provides the functionality of the service but each has its own individual permission and provisioning settings.

Each SPWebApplication object represents a Web application hosted in an Internet Information Services (IIS) Web site. The SPWebApplication object provides access to credentials and other farm-wide application settings. The Sites property gets the collection of site collections within the Web application, and the ContentDatabases property gets the collection of content databases used in the Web application.

An SPContentDatabase object inherits from the SPDatabase class and represents a database that contains user data for a Web application. The Sites property gets the collection of site collections for which the content database stores data, and the WebApplication property gets the parent Web application. An SPSiteCollection object represents the collection of site collections within the Web application.

Site Collections

Definition: A *site collection* is hierarchical set, or collection, of sites. A site collection includes only one top-level site but can contain multiple child sites within. Sites in a site collection share common feature, such as permission, galleries, and Web Parts. Each site collection has a site collection administrator and unique permissions, galleries, and Web Part. This allows a decentralized approach to server farm administration. Within a site collection, a site is used to store content in the form of pages, libraries, and lists. A site can be secured so that only specified users have access to the content of that site.

Subsites in a site collection are sets of sites that share the same owner and administration settings, security, navigation, and content structures. Users and groups can be assigned default rights at the site collection level. Users can be created at any site level and their rights modified at any subsite or item level.

Site Architecture and Object Model Overview

For example, in any organization, there will be several departments such as human resources, administration, production, marketing, and maintenance. Each department may have several subdivisions. So, each division might have its own site collection containing various subsites.

Specifically, the human resource department may have a recruitment division, benefits and compensation division, and a grievances division.

Therefore, the HR department might have its own site collection and top-level site, and each HR subdivision can have individual subsites within the collection. This site and the subsites together form a logical group.

Sites

SharePoint Foundation 2010 comes with many standard templates; however, one of the most commonly used templates is the team site template. A *team site* is a site in SharePoint created using a default site template and is intended to facilitate team collaboration. A team site can have subsites; for instance, specific to various sub-departments of a team. It is the central location to access information and also the location to facilitate communication between team members. Each team site contains basic elements including a title, a logo, navigation tools, and content

The Top-Level or Default Site

In some instances, the team site is the default site or the top-level site. But, a top-level site does not necessarily have to be the team site.

Content Structures

The two most common categories of content structures in a Microsoft SharePoint Foundation site are lists and libraries.

Content Structure	Description
List Stores	individual items such as calendar entries, tasks, contact information, and announcements.
Library	Contains files including documents, pictures, and forms

SharePoint Access Groups

Group	Access Rights
Visitors	Have permissions only to view or read content
Members	Have permissions to read, contribute, modify and delete site content.
Owners	Have same permissions as a member with additional permissions to approve content, create new sites and content structures, and modify the overall site structure.

Permission Levels

Permission levels are rights granted to a user over the content on a SharePoint site.
You can use the default permission levels or create a custom permission level with specific permissions that you want to assign to a group.

The following table describes the various permission levels.

Permission Level	Allows You To
Full Control	Have full control of site content.
Design	View, add, update, delete, approve, and customize content on a site.
Contribute	View, add, update, and delete content on a site.
Read	Only view content only without making any changes.
Limited Access	View specific content when given permission.
Approve	Edit and approve pages, list items, and documents.
Manage Hierarchy	Create sites, and edit pages, list items, and documents
Restricted Read	View pages and documents, but not historical versions or user rights information.

Lesson 1.2

Describe the Team Site Interface Elements

Now that you are familiar with the purpose of Microsoft SharePoint Foundation, the next step is to familiarize yourself with the application and interface elements and navigate around the site. In this topic, you will identify the features of Microsoft SharePoint Foundation team site.

You are an end user of Microsoft SharePoint Foundation team site. In order to access the shared information and communicate effectively with your team members you decide to familiarize yourself with the layout, the navigation tools, and the content structures of a team site.

Interface Elements

SharePoint Foundation 2010 provides an easy-to-use Graphical User Interface (GUI). There are several interface elements in Microsoft SharePoint Foundation 2010.

Interface	Purpose
Ribbon	Enables you to perform simple and advanced operations without having to navigate extensively. It contains the **Navigate Up** button which displays a breadcrumb trail of the pages that you have visited. Therefore, navigating

	through pages becomes faster and easier for anyone who is working in a SharePoint environment. When you access several pages in a SharePoint site, the breadcrumb trail helps you navigate to the parent page easily. The **Edit** button enables you to edit the current page content on a SharePoint team site. This button is most often used while customizing the SharePoint environment. It also contains the **Browse** and the **Page** tabs. In addition to these, it contains the **Site Actions** menu and the **Open Menu** drop-down menu, which is located on the extreme right corner.
The Page Title **link**	Provides a sequential list of links through navigation, from the current page shown on screen to the first page accessed in the site.
The Top Links **bar**	Shows the name of each subsite in a clickable tab across the top of the page. It contains the **Search** text box which enables you to search for content or people on your SharePoint site. The **Help** button on its extreme right corner helps you gain information about the site and the various options available in order to deploy each of them.
The Quick Launch **bar**	Displays links to various lists and libraries. Apart from links to lists and libraries, the **Quick Launch** bar contains links such as **All Site Content** and **Recycle Bin**. When you click the **All Site Content** link, it displays the **All Site**

	Content page, which contains the lists and libraries categorized into groups. In contrast, the **Recycle Bin** enables you to restore or empty deleted items
The Getting Started **section**	The **Getting Started** section contains four links: **Share this site**, **Change site theme**, **Set a site icon** and **Customize the Quick Launch.**
	The **Share this site** link allows site owners and administrators to assign permission levels to users and groups.
	The **Change site theme** link enables you to set the font and color scheme for your site. You can also import new themes to the theme gallery.
	The default themes may include **Mission**, **Vantage**, **Ricasso**, and **Yoshi**. The **Set a site icon** link enables site owners and administrators to set the site title, which is displayed on each page and also the description on the home page. You can also use this option to upload images as logos for your site.
	The **Customize the Quick Launch** link enables site owners and administrators to change links and headings on the **Quick Launch** bar.

The Ribbon

The ribbon provides several components in a SharePoint site that each enable you to perform several operations without having to navigate extensively.

Ribbon Component	Description
The Navigate Up button	Displays a breadcrumb trail of pages that you visited. Therefore, navigating through pages has become faster and easier in a SharePoint environment.
The Edit **button**	Enables you to edit the current page content on a SharePoint team site. This button is most often used while customizing the SharePoint environment.
The Site Actions **menu**	Allows you to edit, format, and align the contents of a page, and create a new page, site, and site components such as lists and libraries. In addition, it allows you to manage permissions and provides you with access to all the settings of a site. Permissions and settings for a site can be configured only by a site owner.
The Open Menu	Enables you to navigate to your personal site, request access for a site, modify user information and settings, change the user sign in, and log out of the site.
The Browse **tab**	Enables you to navigate to the desired page in the Site Hierarchy.

How Create Custom Ribbon

Creating a Custom Ribbon

To create the SharePoint project

1. To start Visual Studio 2010, click the Start Menu, click All Programs, click Microsoft Visual Studio 2010, and then click Microsoft Visual Studio 2010.

2. On the File menu, point to New, and then click Project.

3. In the New Project dialog window, in the Installed Templates section, click Visual C#, click SharePoint, and then click 2010.

4. Click Empty SharePoint Project from the project items.

5. In the Name box, type RibbonDemo and then click OK.

6. In the SharePoint Customization Wizard, type the local Web site that you want to use for this exercise (such as

7. http://localhost/SampleWebSite).

8. For the trust level, select Deploy as a farm solution and then click Finish.

Add the Button Code to the Project

In this task, you add the XML to create the button and ECMAScript (JavaScript, JScript) code to give it functionality.

To add XML code to the project

1. In Solution Explorer, right-click the **RibbonDemo** node, point to **Add**, and then click **New Item**.
2. In the **Add New Item** dialog screen, in the **Installed Templates** section, click **Visual C#**, click **SharePoint**, click **2010**, and then click the **Empty Element** item type.
3. Leave the Name as **EmptyElement1** and then click **OK**.
4. In Solution Explorer, right-click the **EmptyElement1** node and then click **View Code**.
5. Delete the contents of the Elements.xml file.
6. Add the following code to the Elements.xml file.

```
<?xml version="1.0" encoding="utf-8"?>
<Elements
xmlns="http://schemas.microsoft.com/sharepoint/">
<CustomAction
 Id="DemoHelloWorldButton"
 RegistrationType="List"
 RegistrationId="101"
 Location="CommandUI.Ribbon">
  <CommandUIExtension>
    <CommandUIDefinitions>
     <CommandUIDefinition

Location="Ribbon.Documents.New.Controls._children">
<Button

Id="Ribbon.Documents.New.Controls.DemoHelloWorldB
utton"
```

```
            Alt="Hello World Ribbon Button"
            Sequence="10"
            Image32by32="/_layouts/images/PPEOPLE.GIF"
            Command="Demo_HelloWorld"
            LabelText="Hello World Demo"
            TemplateAlias="o2"/>
         </CommandUIDefinition>
       </CommandUIDefinitions>
       <CommandUIHandlers>
         <CommandUIHandler
          Command="Demo_HelloWorld"
          CommandAction="javascript:alert('HelloWorld!');"
/>
       </CommandUIHandlers>
      </CommandUIExtension>
     </CustomAction>
    </Elements>
```

The TemplateAlias attribute defines whether a medium (o2)
or large (o1) button is displayed. The CommandAction
element contains the ECMAScript (JavaScript, JScript) code
that runs when you press the button.

Deploy and Test the Solution

In this task, you deploy the solution and then verify that the
button is displayed on the ribbon. Then you click the button
to display the dialog box.

To test the solution

1. In Solution Explorer, right-click the **RibbonDemo**
    node and then click **Deploy**.

2. Start Internet Explorer and browse to the Web site
    specified previously.

3. In the left navigation pane, click **Shared Documents** to open the Shared Documents library.

4. Click the **Documents** tab in the SharePoint 2010 ribbon.

   a. You should see the new **Hello World Demo** button added to the ribbon.

5. Click **Hello World Demo**. The Hello World JavaScript dialog box appears as shown Figure 1.

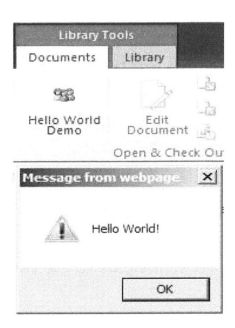

Remove the Button

In this task, you remove the **Hello World Demo** button.

To remove the button:

1. In Solution Explorer, right-click the **EmptyElement1** node and then click **View Code**.

2. Comment the existing code by typing **<!--** in front of the opening **<CustomAction>** element. Next, type --> after the closing **</CustomAction>** element.

3. After the commented code, insert the following code.

   ```
   <HideCustomAction
   Id="Ribbon.Documents.New.Controls.DemoHell
   oWorldButton"
   Location="Ribbon.Documents.New.Controls._c
   hildren"> </HideCustomAction>
   ```

4. Deploy and test the updated solution by following steps 1 through 4 in Task 3, Deploy and Test.

You should see that the **Hello World Demo** button is no longer displayed on the ribbon.

The Quick Launch Bar

The **Quick Launch** bar provides several components that each enable you to navigate to the various pages in the site quickly.

Component	Description
Links to List and Libraries	Displays links to various lists and libraries in the site. While creating a list or library, you can specify options that enable you to display the list or library

	on the **Quick Launch** bar.
The All Site Content **link**	Displays the **All Site Content** page, which contains the lists and libraries categorized as groups.
The Recycle Bin **link**	Enables you to restore or empty deleted items. The *Recycle Bin* in a SharePoint Foundation site is similar to your Windows Recycle Bin

The Getting Started Section

The **Getting Started** section has several components that enable you to customize the appearance and navigation of the site.

Component	Description
The Share this site **link**	Allows site owners and administrators to assign permission levels to users and groups.
The Change site theme **link**	Enables you to set the font and color scheme for your site. You can also import new themes to the themes gallery.
The Set a site icon **link**	Enables site owners and administrators to set the site title, which is displayed on each page, and the description, which is displayed on the home page. You can also use this option to upload images as logos for your site.
Customize the Quick	Enables site owners and administrators to change links and headings on the **Quick Launch** bar.

Lesson 1 Follow-up

In this lesson, you examined collaboration technology and Microsoft SharePoint Foundation team sites. With a solid understanding of the technology, you can begin integrating the features of SharePoint sites into your current work environment.

1. **How would using a collaboration technology like Microsoft SharePoint Foundation 2010 instead of traditional email allow your team to be more efficient?**

   Answers will vary, but may include: Facilitates efficient organization and information storage for project teams or departments and also facilitates easy information availability to team members spread across geographical locations. SharePoint Foundation 2010 provides specialized sites that can be used as a powerful collaborative tool and help to drive productivity by offering a host of functionalities that include central calendar, task lists, discussion boards, wikis, blogs, libraries of documents, photos, and forms.

2. **Which navigation element would you use frequently to access content? Why?**

   *Answers will vary, but may include: The **Navigate Up** icon because it enables you to navigate to the parent site without having to click the **Back** button on the browser several times; the **Quick Launch** bar because it helps you to access content on a site easily; and the breadcrumb because it helps you navigate to the sites visited in the site hierarchy.*

Chapter 2

Working with Lists

In this lesson, you will add and modify list items and work with list views.

You will:

- ✓ Add items to Microsoft SharePoint Foundation lists.
- ✓ Modify list items.
- ✓ Change list views.

Introduction

You have learned how to navigate within a team site and now you want to begin participating in the collaboration environment. Lists are one of the most common types of information that appears on team sites. In this lesson, you will work with lists in SharePoint Foundation.

Within each site, you can provision lists, libraries, and pages. A list is the basic type of object inside SharePoint Foundation. There are different kinds of lists. Some of the list types include announcement lists, task lists, and event lists. Lists contain columns of information that are often referred to as fields. You can define custom columns to suit the kind of data that you want to store in a list. And you can use columns to sort, filter, and group list items. A document library is a specialized kind of list that is used to store files and folders. The columns in a document library are used to store metadata about a document.

Lesson 2.1

List Items

In this lesson, you will work with lists. Before you can access list information, someone has to create it and place it at the appropriate location. In this topic, you will add items to the lists in your team site.

Almost everyone has a list or two floating around with information they use on a regular basis.

The lists are written on a piece of paper, stored as a document on a computer, or saved in an email message. Each time the information changes, you have to get out the eraser or whiteout to change the hard copy, or make changes and resend an email message. Instead of going through that tedious process, you can add information to lists on a team site where the information can be updated once and available for use by everyone on the team.

Definition: A SharePoint *list* is a content structure that contains a group of similar items. There are different types of lists, and a team site can contain multiple lists of a similar or different type. Each site contains a set of default lists such as calendar, tasks, links, and announcements. The site owner can add other lists, if required.

Types of Lists

There are various types of lists in a SharePoint Foundation+

List Type	Description
Announcements	Displays short information items such as recent news or status updates
Calendar	Keeps track of team meetings, events, and holidays in a familiar calendar view
Links	Displays a list of links from the Internet or your company intranet.
Tasks	Stores action items for your team or a project.
Review	Enables you to track the software issues

	related to a type of list by assigning it to a user along with its priority level.
Contacts	Contains contact information for individuals and groups, such as clients or vendors.
Project tasks	Stores task items for a single project and provides summary info in a **Gantt** view with progress bars. A **Gantt** view is a view format type where data is displayed in a graphical format along with progress bars.
Issue tracking	Follows the progress of an issue of one or more items that are not project-related, such as support issues.
	Facilitates multiple discussions and newsgroups related to the organization.
	Enables tracking and recording user responses to specific list of questions, thereby enabling organization to collect user preferences or data.

How Create A List

In this task, you crete the list and add the custom content types.

To Create a List:

1. Start Internet Explorer and browse to the Web site where you have created the new content type.

2. In the upper-left corner of the page, click **Site Actions** and then click **More Options**.

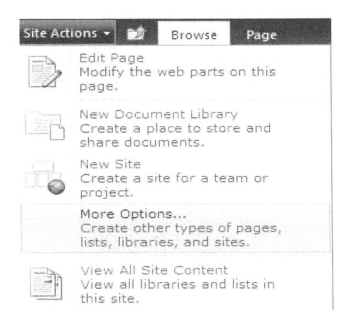

3. Click **List** in the **Filter By** menu in the **Create** dialog screen.

4. Select **Custom List**.

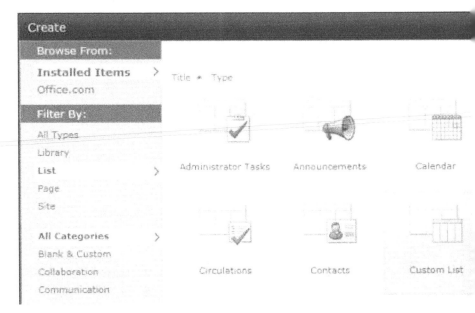

5. Type **New Announcements** as the name and then click **Create**.

6. Click **List Settings** in the SharePoint 2010 ribbon and then under **General Settings**, click **Advanced settings**.

7. Click **Yes** for **Allow management of content types** and then click **OK**.

8. Under the **Content Types** section, click the **Item** content type.

9. Under **Settings**, click **Delete this content type**.

10. If prompted for confirmation, select **OK**.

11. Under the **Content Types** section, click **Add from existing site content types**.

12. From the available site content types list, click **New Announcements** and then click **Add**.

13. Click **OK**. You should now see the **New Announcements** content type associated with the **New Announcements** list.

Content Types

This list is configured to allow multiple content types. Use content type addition to its policies, workflows, or other behavior. The following cor

Content Type	Visible on New Button
New Announcements	✔

14. Click the **New Announcements** list item.

15. Scroll down to the **Columns** section and verify that there is a **Team Project** and **Company** column.

How to Add List Items

Add an Item to the Announcements List

To add an item to the **Announcements** list:

1. On the **Quick Launch** bar, click the **Lists** link.

2. On the **All Site content** page, in the **Lists** section, click the **Announcements** link.

3. On the **Announcements: All Items** page, click the **Add new announcement** link.

4. In the **Announcements - New Items** dialog box, in the **Title** text box, enter the title of the announcement.

5. If necessary, in the **Body** text box, enter the body text.

6. In the **Expires** text box, click the **Date Picker** icon to select an expiration date.

7. Click **Save.**

Generally, only the five most recent announcements are displayed on the home page. If you select an expiration date, then the announcement is displayed on the home page until that date. After the expiration date, you can access the announcement from the **All Items** view on the **Announcements** page.

Add a Calendar Entry

To add a calendar entry to a team calendar:

1. On the **Quick Launch** bar, click the **Calendar** link.
2. On the **Events** tab, in the **New** group, click **New event.**
3. On the **Calendar-New Item** page, in the **Title** text box, enter a title for the event.
4. If necessary, in the **Location** text box, type the location of the event.
5. In the **Start Time** text box, click the **Date Picker** icon to enter the start date and time.
6. In the **End Time** text box, click the **Date Picker** icon to enter the end date and time.
7. If necessary, in the **Description** text box, type a description for the event.
8. If necessary, select a **Category** for the new event.
9. Select the **Category** option to select a type of category.
10. Or, select the **Specify your own value** option to enter a value of your choice.
11. If necessary, check the **All Day Event** check box to make the current event an all-day event without a specific start or end time.
12. If necessary, check the **Recurrence** check box and specify the following:

    - Select a frequency (daily, monthly, weekly, yearly).
    - Select a pattern (once a week, bi-monthly, etc.).

- Select a start date.

11. Click **Save.**

Add a Link

To add a link to a website:

1. On the **Quick Launch** bar, click the **Lists** link to display the lists.
2. On the **All Site Content** page, click the **Links** link.
3. On the **Links — All Links** page, click the **Add new link** link.

   If you want to be sure the web address you entered for a link is correct, use the **Click Here To Test** link. This will save you the trouble of opening an Internet browser and entering the link to see if it works.

4. In the **Links — New Item** dialog box, in the **URL** text box, enter the address.

   If you enter a description, this text will be used as the link instead of the web address.

5. If desired, in the **Notes** text box, enter any notes and then click **Save.**
6. If necessary, click the **Click Here To Test** link to confirm if the web address entered for a link is correct.

Add a Task

To add an item to the task list or a project task list:

69

1. On the **Quick Launch** bar, click the **Tasks** link or the name of the task list.

2. On the **Tasks — All Tasks** page, click the **Add new item** link.

3. In the **Tasks-New Item** dialog box, in the **Title** text box, enter a title for the task, and if necessary, click **Add** to add a predecessor to the existing task item.

4. If necessary, from the **Priority** drop-down list, select a priority level option to mention the priority for the task, and from the **Status** drop-down list, select a status level option to mention the status of task.

5. If necessary, in the **% Complete** text box, type a value that indicates the amount of work completed.

6. If necessary, in the **Assigned To** text box, enter a name to assign the task.

   - Click the **Check Names** icon to verify if the name is typed correctly.
   - Click the **Book** icon to browse for the name in the directory.

7. If necessary, in the **Description** text box, enter a description.

8. If necessary, in the **Start Date** text box, click the **Date Picker** icon to enter a start date, and in the **Due Date** text box, enter a due date.

9. Click Save

Lesson 1.2

Modify List Items

Now that you have added content to lists, you will invariably find you need to edit the information. In this topic, you will modify list items. A team site would quickly become useless if you are not able to make any changes to the content.

Using the most current information available is crucial to the collaborative environment. Microsoft SharePoint Foundation enables you to update information and have the updated information available to team members immediately.

List Modification Options

List modification options available on a Microsoft SharePoint Foundation team site will enable you to edit list items. There are two list modification options.

How to Modify List Items

Modify a List Item

To modify a list item:

1. On the **Quick Launch** bar, click the **All Site Content** link.

2. On the **All Site Content** page, select the list in which you have to modify an item.

3. Switch to the **All <items>** view.

4. To modify an item:

    a. On the **<List name>– All items** page, select the desired item.
    b. On the **Items** tab, click **Edit Item.**
    c. On the **<List name>– <Item name>** dialog box, modify the essential details and click **Save**.

On most items, you can also hover over the item and then click the drop-down arrow and choose **Edit Item** from the menu.

Lesson **1.3**

Change List Views

In previous topics, you worked with list items in the standard list view format. If you would like to see the information displayed differently, you can select a different way to view the list. In this topic, you will change a list view.

Lists are a great way to organize information, but one long list can be a lot of information to process all at once. After you've looked at a couple of lists for a few hours, everything seems to look the same. In order to access list information more quickly, you can choose to view lists in different formats and display only the information you want.

List Views

A *list view* is a format for displaying items in a list. Each list has at least one default view that shows all the items in the list. Some lists have more than one view. Other views are available, depending on the type of list being displayed. You can change to a different view at any time without affecting the information in a list.

How to Change List Views

Switch a List View to Datasheet View

To switch a list view to the Datasheet view:

1. On the **Quick Launch** bar, in the **Lists** section, select the type of list.

2. On the **<List name>** page, on the **List** tab, click **Create View.**

3. On the **Create View** page, in the **Choose a view format** section, click **Datasheet View**.

4. On the **Create Datasheet View page**, in the **Name** section, in the Name text box, enter the desired name.

5. If necessary, in the **Audience** section, under **View Audience**, select the type of audience to create the view.

6. If necessary, in the **Columns** section, check all the required options that need to be displayed to select or be hidden in the **Datasheet** view.

7. If necessary, in the **Sort** section, specify the desired sort options.

   ✓ From the **First sort by column** drop-down list, choose the default **none** option to sort the columns in which the items in the view are displayed.

   ✓ Or, choose one or more columns based on which you want to sort the items in the list.

8. From the **First sort by the column** drop-down list, select the desired primary column based on which you want to sort the items.

9. From the **Then sort by the column** drop-down list, select the desired secondary column based on which you want to sort the items.

10. In the **Filters** section, choose an option to show all items or display only a subset of items in this type of view.

11. In the **Totals** section, under **Column Name,** from the necessary drop-down list, select the options that best suit your requirements.

12. In the **Folders** section, under the **Folders or Flat** option, choose an option to specify the folders through which you can navigate to view the items in the list.

13. If necessary, in the **Item Limit** section, under **Number of items to display**, choose an option to limit the amount of data that users can view.

14. Click **OK**

Switch a List Item View to Calendar View

To switch a list item to a Calendar view:

1. On the **Quick Launch** bar, in the **Lists** section, select the type of list.

2. On the **<List name>** page, on the **List** tab, click **Create View.**

3. On the **Create View** page, in the **Choose a view format** section, click **Calendar View.**

4. On the **Create Calendar View** page, in the **Name** section, in the **View Name** text box, enter a name.

5. If necessary, in the **Audience** section, under **View Audience**, select the type of audience to create the view.

6. In the **Time Interval** section, select the desired time interval.

   ✓ From the **Begin** drop-down list, choose a start time to specify the start time for those columns required to place items in the calendar.

   ✓ From the **End** drop-down list, choose an end time to specify the end time for those columns required to place items in the calendar.

7. In the **Calendar Columns** section, select the desired calendar columns.

   ✓ From the **Month View Title** drop-down list, choose an option to specify columns under the month view.

   ✓ From the **Week View Title** drop-down list, choose an option to specify columns under the weeks view.
   ✓ From the **Week View Sub Heading** drop-down list, choose an option to specify columns under the week view sub heading.

   ✓ From the **Day View Title** drop-down list, choose an option to specify columns under the day view.

   ✓ From the **Day View Sub Heading** drop-down list, choose an option to specify columns under the day view sub heading.

76

8.   In the **Default Scope** section, from the **Default Scope** options, choose an option to specify the default scope for the view.

9.   In the **Filter** section, select a type of filter to show all items in the list or a subset of lists.

10. In the **Mobile** section, select an option to adjust mobile settings for this view.

11. Click **OK.**

Switch a List Item View to Gantt View

To switch to a Gantt view:

1.   On the **Quick Launch** bar, in the **Lists** section, select the type of list.

2.   On the **<List name>** page, on the **List** tab, click **Create View.**

3.   On the **Create View** page, on the **Choose a view format** section, click **Gantt View.**

4.   On the **Create View** page, in the **Name** section, in the **View Name** text box, enter the desired name.

5.   In the **Audience** section, from the **View Audience** option, select the type of audience to create the view.

6.   In the **Columns** section, select the columns that you need to show or hide in the gantt view.

7. In the **Gantt columns** section, choose the desired columns that are to be presented in the Gantt chart.

   ✓ From the **Title** drop-down list, choose an option to specify the title for the column text field.

   ✓ From the **Start Date** drop-down list, select an option to specify the start date for the column list.

   ✓ From the **Due Date** drop-down list, select an option to specify the due date for the column.

   ✓ From the **Percent Complete** drop-down list, select an option to specify the percent of task completed for the column.

   ✓ From the **Predecessors** drop-down list, select an option to specify the predecessors for the column.

8. In the **Sort** section, specify the desired sort options.

   ✓ From the **First sort by column** drop-down list, choose the default **none** option to sort the columns in which the items in the view are displayed.

   ✓ Or, choose one or more columns based on which you want to sort the items in the list.

1. From the **First sort by the column** drop-down list, select the desired primary column based on which you want to sort the items.

2. From the **Then sort by the column** drop-down list, select the desired secondary column based on which you want to sort the items.

3. In the **Filter** section, select a type of filter to show all items in the list or a subset of lists.

4. In the **Group By** section, select an option to determine the way in which the items in the list will be displayed in groups and subgroups.

5. In the **Totals** section, select one or more totals to display. In the **Style** section, from the **View Style** list box, choose an option to represent the style for this view.

6. In the **Folders** section, under the **Folders or Flat** option, choose an option to specify the folders through which you can navigate to view the items in the list.

7. Under **Show this view** option, choose an option to display the current view in the suitable location.

8. In the **Item Limit** section, under **Number of items to display**, choose an option to limit the amount of data that users can view.

9. Click **OK.**

Switch a List Item View to Standard View

To switch to Standard view:

1. On the **Quick Launch** bar, in the **Lists** section, select the type of list.

2. On the **<List name>** page, on the **List** tab, click **Create View.**

3. On the **Create View** page, on the **Choose a view format** page, click **Standard View.**

4. On the **Create View** page, in the **Name** section, in the **View Name** text box, enter a name.

5. In the **Audience** section, from the **View Audience** option, select the type of audience to create the view.

6. In the **Columns** section, select the columns that you need to show or hide in the standard view.

7. In the Sort section, specify the desired sort options.

    ✓   From the **First sort by column** drop-down list, choose the default **none** option to sort the columns in which the items in the view are displayed.

    ✓   Or, choose one or more columns based on which you want to sort the items in the list.

8. From the **First sort by the column** drop-down list, select the desired primary column based on which you want to sort the items.
9. From the **Then sort by the column** drop-down list, select the desired secondary column based on which you want to sort the items.
10. In the **Filter** section, select a type of filter to show all items in the list or a subset of lists.
11. In the **Inline Editing** section, check Allow inline editing to display an edit icon in each row so that you can edit the current row in the view without navigating to the form.

12. If necessary, choose **Tabular View** to provide individual check boxes to the items to each row.

13. In the **Group By** section, select an option to determine the way in which the items in the list will be displayed in groups and subgroups.

14. If necessary, in the **Totals** section, select one or more totals to display.

15. If necessary, in the **Style** section, from the **View Style** list box, choose an option to represent the style for this view.

16. If necessary, in the **Folders** section, under Folders or Flat, choose an option to specify the folders through which you can navigate to view the items in the list.

17. If necessary, in the **Item Limit** section, under **Number of items to display**, choose an option to limit the amount of data that users can view.

18. If necessary, in the **Mobile** section, select an option to adjust mobile settings for this view.

19. Click **OK.**

Change Calendar Settings

To change calendar settings:

1. In a SharePoint calendar, on the ribbon, on the **Calendar** tab, in the **Settings** group, click **List Settings.**

2. In the **General Settings** section, click the **Title, description and navigation** link.

3. In the **Group Calendar Options** section, under **Use this calendar to share member's schedules,** select **Yes** to create events in the calendar with attendees.

4. Click **Save**

Lesson 2 Follow-up

In this lesson, you worked with different types of lists. You added items, modified the list items, and also changed the view format of the items in the list. This will enable you to work with information in the lists in your team site. Shared information containing organized lists, enables users to efficiently locate information stored across the team site.

1. **Besides Contacts and Announcements, which lists would you and your team use the most? Why?**

    Answers will vary, but may include: The tasks list will be used to store information related to the various tasks that the organization needs to perform on a monthly basis. The Discussion Board list is also one that many teams use often, and which will make information sharing and conversations among team members easier and faster.

2. Which list would you modify often? Why?

Answers will vary, but may include: Tasks lists will be modified often as information pertaining to the team changes frequently. Therefore, users need to modify those items in the list. You can also use the calendar list to update your schedule.

Chapter 3

Working with Libraries

In this lesson, you will add, edit, and share documents across libraries and wikis.
You will:

- ✓ Add documents to a library.
- ✓ Edit library documents.
- ✓ Share documents across libraries.
- ✓ Create wiki pages.
- ✓ Request access to a specific SharePoint resource.

Introduction

In the previous lesson, you worked with content in various types of SharePoint lists, one of the most common types of SharePoint content structures. Libraries are another common type of content structure, which enables you to collaborate with team members using larger files. In this lesson, you will work with libraries.

Lists are an ideal way of keeping track of numerous small pieces of information, but eventually you will need a place to store documents, photos, forms, and other large chunks of data.

Rather than attempting to access documents from numerous locations including your computer hard drive, various network locations, and possibly hundreds of email messages, a SharePoint library provides a central location for team members to store all their necessary files.

Lesson 3.1

Add Documents to a Library

In this lesson, you will work with libraries. Just as you need to populate lists with content before performing other list tasks, you also need to populate libraries with the files that you need to share with the rest of your team before doing further work in the library. In this topic, you will add documents to a library.

One of the most challenging aspects of working in a team is to locate files quickly. Files are often stored in numerous locations, including the network, individual hard drives, and removable media like thumb drives. With information available in different locations, it is easy to overlook important documents or waste valuable time in creating a document that exists. In contrast, if you can both upload existing documents and create new team documents in a SharePoint library, you will have one location for every file in your SharePoint team site.

SharePoint Libraries

Definition: A *SharePoint library* is a content structure that is used to store files. A library may contain a single type of file, such as a picture library, or it may contain multiple types of files including documents, spreadsheets, and presentations. A default SharePoint library, **Shared Documents**, is created automatically when a new team site is created.

Although the **Shared Documents** library can contain multiple file types, pictures, forms, and wiki pages are generally stored in separate libraries. A site owner can create additional libraries as needed

Library Folders

You can create folders in most libraries. This allows you to organize files effectively in groups rather than show all files in the library as one long list.

Add Library Folder to Library

To add a folder to a library:

1. Login to your SharePoint site as the administrative account
2. Select Site Actions > View All Site Content

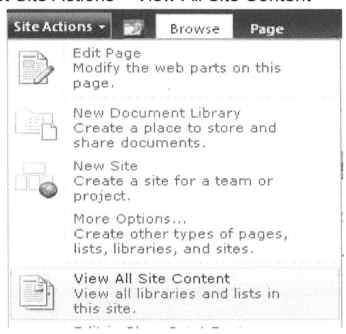

3. Select the Document Library in which you want to add the folder

4. In the Ribbon under the Library Tools Section click Document Tab

5. Click New Folder under the New Group.

New
Folder

6. Enter New Folder Name

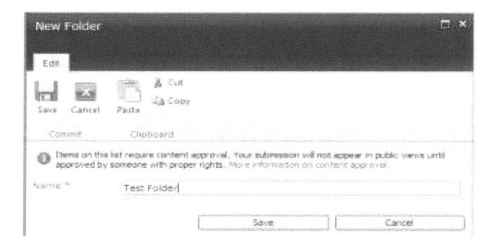

7. Click Save

Types of Libraries

There are four library types available in SPF 2010.

Library Type	Purpose
Document	Usually contains files such as documents, spreadsheets, and presentations. New files created in this library are limited to a single type of file (i.e. Word, Excel, PowerPoint) which is chosen when the library is created by the site owner. However, any

	type of file can be uploaded to this library.
Picture	Primarily contains pictures displayed as thumbnails. Pictures can be uploaded to the library but not created directly within the library. Specialized viewing and download options are available in addition to basic file storage.
Form	Stores XML-based (eXtensible Markup Language) forms such as invoices and expense reports used by programs such as Microsoft InfoPath.
Wiki Page	Contains linked wiki pages and supports text, pictures, tables, and hyperlinks embedded on those pages.

Microsoft InfoPath is a program that enables efficient information gathering by providing an easy-to-do form filling in procedures that help while working with email, web browsers, or mobile devices.

Ways to Populate Libraries

Depending on how the library is configured, there are several options for placing documents into a library, including:

— Uploading from your computer,
— The network or other media.
— Creating them directly in the library within the SharePoint environment.

How to Add Documents to a Library

Upload Files to a Document Library

To upload files to a document library:

1.   On the **Quick Launch** bar, click a document library link.

2.   On the **<Library name> - All Documents** page, on the **Documents** tab, in the **New** group, choose **Upload Document** or **Upload Multiple Documents**.

If you chose **Upload Document:**

a.   On the **<Library name - Upload Document** dialog box, click **Browse.**

b.   In the **Choose File** dialog box, browse to the location of the file that you want to upload.

c.   Select the file.

d.   Click **Open.**

e.   If necessary, uncheck **Overwrite existing files.**

f.   Click **OK.**

If you chose **upload Multiple Documents:**

a.   On the **<Library name - Upload Multiple Documents** dialog box, on the left pane, click the **Browse for files instead** link to browse the location of the file or files.

b. On the right pane, check the files that you want to upload.

c. Click **Open** to upload the selected files.

d. If necessary, uncheck **Overwrite existing files.**

e. Click **OK.**

Upload Files to a Picture Library

To upload picture files to a picture library:

1. Click a picture library link.

2. On the **Documents** tab, in the **New** group, choose **Upload Picture** or **Upload Multiple Pictures.**

If you chose **Upload Picture:**

a. In the **Select Picture** dialog box, click **Browse.**
b. In the **Choose File** dialog box, browse to the location of the file that\ you want to upload.
c. Select the file.
d. Click **Open.**
e. If necessary, uncheck **Overwrite existing files.**
f. Click **OK.** The **Edit Item** page opens, where you can add or modify properties such as File Name, Title, Date Picture Taken, Description, Keywords.
g. Click **OK.**

If you chose **Upload Multiple Pictures:**

a. If necessary, in the **Microsoft Office Picture Manager** window, browse to the location of the picture files.

b. Select the picture files that you want to upload.

c. Click **Upload And Close.**

d. When the **Uploading Pictures** page is displayed, click the **Go Back To <LibraryName>** link.

Create Documents in the Shared Documents Library

To create documents in the Shared Documents library:

1. On the **Quick Launch** bar, click the **Shared Documents** link.

2. On the **Shared Documents - All Documents** page, on the **Documents** tab, in the

3. **New** group, click **New Document.**

4. To acknowledge the security message and open Microsoft Office Word 2010, click

5. **OK.** The application opens in Compatibility Mode.

6. Enter the text and other content for the new document, and format it as necessary.

7. Click **Save.** By default, the file will be saved in the Shared Documents folder on the SharePoint server.

8. Type a file name and click **Save.**

Creating Documents in Other Libraries

Creating documents in other libraries is similar to creating documents in the **Shared Documents** library, but the specific steps depend on the configuration of the library itself. For instance, if a document library is configured so that its template is a Microsoft Excel spreadsheet, then Excel will open when you click **New Document.**

Lesson 3.2

Edit Library Documents

Now that your team has files stored in a SharePoint library, it is likely that team members will need to make changes to the files. You will need to work without overwriting each other's efforts. In this topic, you will use file versioning and check out and check in as you edit library files so that you can collaborate on content without creating conflicting versions.

If every team member could make changes to a file at the same time, the latest and the most accurate change might not be known. When members are required to check out files in order
to edit them, an orderly sequence of changes is created, and each member can make sure that their changes are not lost or overwritten.

Versions

Definition: *Versions* are successive copies of a document that are created each time the file is modified. A version number is assigned to each copy. The version number, a description of the modification, and the date the file was modified are all visible in the document library. Using versions allows a file to be reverted back to an earlier copy or recovered if it is accidentally deleted. Versioning is not enabled in SharePoint by default, but it can be enabled by the site owner. Versioning can be enabled on both lists and libraries.

Major vs. Minor Versions

Versions are classified as either major (for example, adding, changing, or deleting large sections of text) or minor (for example, updating few figures in a spreadsheet or changing the wording of a sentence). Major versions are indicated by whole numbers (1.0, 2.0, 3.0, etc.), while minor versions are indicated by decimals (1.1, 1.2, 1.3, etc.).

The Check In/Check Out Process

The Check In/Check Out process enables you to take a document out of the library, make the required changes, and put the document back into the library for other users. It prevents multiple users from editing the same file simultaneously. Each time a file is checked out, it is locked and other users can read the file but cannot edit it. The Check In/Check Out process involves a series of activities.

1. Identify the file in a library that you want to check out.
2. Once team member checks out a file, it is locked.
3. The team member makes changes and saves the file.
4. The file is checked in, and if versioning is enabled, a new version number is created.
5. And, the file is unlocked.

Editing vs. Checking Out

You can modify a file in a library either by editing it directly or by checking it out and then editing the content. If versioning is enabled on a library, each time you save a file while you are editing it directly, a version is automatically created. It does not matter how simple or complex the change is, once any change is made and the document saved, a version is assigned. In contrast, when you check out a file, you can edit and save the changes locally as many times as you want without creating new versions. A new version is not created until you check the file back in to the library.

How to Edit Library Documents

Open a Read-Only Copy of a Library File

To open a read-only copy of a library file:

1. On the **Quick Launch** bar, click the desired library link to navigate to the library that holds the file you want to open.
2. Click the name of the file that you want to open.

3. In the **Open Document** dialog box, verify that **Read Only** is selected, and click

Open a Library File for Editing

To open a library file for editing:

1. On the **Quick Launch** bar, click the desired library link to navigate to the library that holds the file you want to open.

2. Click the name of the file you want to open.

3. In the **Open Document** dialog box, click **Edit** and click **OK.**

4. When the application and file have opened, make necessary changes..

5. Save and close the file.

Check Out a File

To check out a file:

1. Navigate to the library that holds the document you need to check out.

2. Check the file that you want to check out.

3. On the Documents tab, in the **Open & Checkout** group, click **Check Out.**

4. In the Comments area you may wish to add a comment that describes the changes you made for revision tracking purposes.

5. In the **Microsoft Internet Explorer** message box, check **Use my local drafts folder** and click **OK.**

6. Open **My Documents** and double-click **SharePoint Drafts** to display the checked-out file.**OK.**

Check In a File

To check out a file:

1. Navigate to the library that holds the document you need to check out.

2. Check the file that you want to check In or Right Click on the File Properties.

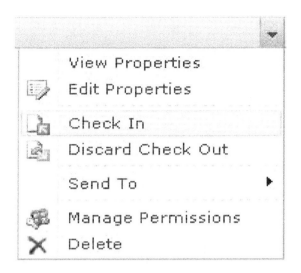

3. **Click Ok**

Check In a File

To discard a check-out:

1. Login to your SharePoint site as the administrative account
2. Select Site Actions > View All Site Content

3. Select your Document Library

4. Click the drop-down arrow next to the file you want to check in and select Discard Check Out

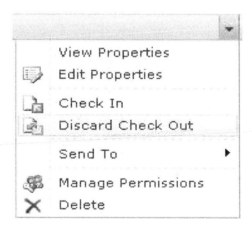

5. Click OK

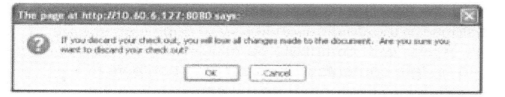

Lesson 3.3

Share Documents across Libraries

Now, you may want to share the library documents that you've been working on with specific team members. You may need to enable options that can facilitate sharing of sensitive documents across different libraries as per the business needs of your organization. In this topic, you will share documents across libraries.

An organization consists of many departments, and certain documents such as job applications might require processing from many other departments. You may need to enable the options provided in Microsoft SharePoint Foundation 2010 so that documents in a library can be shared with other libraries.

The Send to Command

The **Send To** command is used to copy a file from a library to another location. The **Send To** command also enables you to copy files between libraries and it can be accessed from a file's shortcut menu. It provides options to send the file link as email, create a document workspace, and download the file. The user should have the **Contribute** permissions for the destination library to copy files among libraries. A user with contribute permission will be able to view and update contents in a library, add contents to a library, and delete contents from a library.

How to Share Documents across Libraries

Add a Send to Destination for a Document Library

To add a **Send To** destination for a document library:

This can be configured only by the site owner.

1. Open the desired document library.

2. On the **Library** tab, in the **Settings** group, click **Library Settings** to navigate to the **Document Library Settings** page.

3. In the **General Settings** section, click **Advanced settings.**

4. On the **Advanced Settings** page, in the **Custom Send To Destination** section, in the **Destination name** text box, enter the desired library name.

5. In the **URL** text box, enter the desired URL for the document library.

6. On the **Advanced Settings** page, click **OK.**

Copy a File to a Predefined Destination

To copy a file to a predefined destination:

1. Open the desired library.

2. Open the drop-down menu of the desired file and mouse over the **Send To** option and choose the desired location.

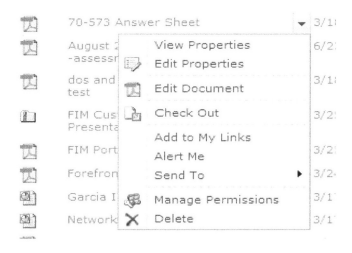

*To be able to copy a file and share it across libraries by sending it to a predefined location, the **Send To** destination has to be enabled by the site owner. Once this option is enabled, an end user will be able to copy files to any **Send To** predefined destination.*

3. If necessary, on the **Copy: <file name>** page, in the **Destination** section, modify the

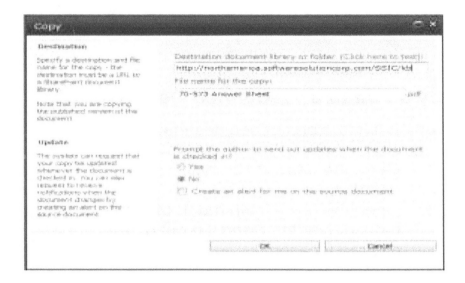

4. destination URL and rename the file.

5. If necessary, in the **Update** section, select **Yes.**

6. If necessary, in the **Update** section, check the **Create an alert for me on the source document** check box.

7. On the **Copy: <file name>** page, click **OK.**

8. In the **Copy Progress** dialog box, click **OK.**

9. In the **Copy Progress** dialog box, click **Done.**

Update Copies from a Source File

To update copies from a source file:

1. Open the library containing the source file.

2. On the Documents tab, in the **Copies group**, choose **Send To, Existing Copies** button.

3. On the **Update Copies: <file name>** page, in the **Destinations** section, check the desired check boxes.
4. In the **Copy Progress** dialog box, click **OK.**
5. In the **Copy Progress** dialog box, click **Done.**

Update Copies from the Manage Copies Page

To update copies from the **Manage Copies** page:

1. Access the desired destination library.
2. Click the desired file.
3. On the Documents tab, in the **Copies** group, click **Manage Copies.**
4. In the **Manage Copies** dialog box, click **Update Copies.**
5. In the **Update Copies** dialog box, in the **Destinations** section, check the desired check boxes.
6. In the **Copy Progress** dialog box, click **OK.**
7. In the **Copy Progress** dialog box, click **Done.**

Lesson 3.4

Create Wiki Pages

In the previous topic, you shared files across libraries to centralize critical information or data. Another way to capture information from your team is to add it to a wiki. In this topic, you will create wiki pages.

SharePoint lists contain short information items, while SharePoint libraries contain entire files of information. But what do you do with information that is bigger than a list item and not quite an entire file? What about the knowledge your team members are aware of but doesn't seem to be documented anywhere? A SharePoint wiki provides a method to capture the collective information of all team members so nothing important is overlooked or lost.

Wikis

Definition: A *wiki* is a collection of web pages that contain information created by an online community. It is a user-created knowledge base in which users add and modify content as they wish. Wikis are generally not limited to any particular subject or size. Although various levels of administration can be implemented, by default a wiki can be updated by any user who has access. A wiki can be either limited to a particular subject based on the organization's needs, or extended to include various subjects. A wiki is a dynamic content repository since it is updated continually.

Wiki Technology

Wiki technology, including the Wiki markup language, is less than 20 years old. In that time, wiki-based content sites have become some of the most useful as well as the most controversial on the web, because of their open-ended, community-based approach to documentation and information sharing. You can read more about wikis and their history at one of the best-known wikis, Wikipedia, at **http://en.wikipedia.org/wiki/Wikis**.

Wiki Syntax

Wiki documents are web pages and use standard HTML web syntax, although most wikis provide a What You See Is What You Get (WYSIWYG) HTML editing tool. In addition, many wikis support some type of wiki-specific markup language or syntax, which you can use to create *wiki links* or free links between pages or between sections of a page in the wiki. Generally, these links use square bracket pairs with the target page or section name within the brackets.

How to Create Wiki Page Library

Create a Wiki Page Library

1. Select Site Actions > More Options

2. Scroll down and Click Wiki Page Library

Wiki Page Library

3.   Enter a Name for the Library

Wiki Page Library

Type: Library
Categories: Collaboration, Content

An interconnected set of easily editable
web pages, which can contain text,
images and web parts.

Wiki Links|

[Create] [More Options]

4.   Click Create

How to Create Wiki Pages

Create a Wiki Page

To create a wiki page:

1.   In the **Quick Launch** bar, click the name of the wiki that
     you want to edit.
2.   On the wiki's **Home** page, on the Ribbon, click the **Edit**
     button.

3.   Create a link for the new page.
4.   Place the cursor where you want the link to appear.
5.   Type the name of the new page in double brackets; for
     example, ***[[Expense Reports]]***.
6.   If necessary, enter the pipe symbol (|) and a title for the
     link; for example

[[Expense Reports | Submitting Expense Reports]].

7. On the **Format Text** tab, click **Save & Close.**
8. On the **Home** page, click the new page link.
9. In the **New Page** message box, click **Create.**
10. On the new wiki page, add the necessary content, including text, graphics, links to other pages, and so forth.
11. Format the text and other content as necessary.
12. Click the **Save** button.

How to Edit Wiki Pages

Edit a Wiki Page

1. Login to your SharePoint site as the administrative account

2. Select Site Actions > All Site Content

    3.

4. Select the wiki library you want to edit

5. Click Edit on the wiki page you want to edit

6.   Edit the text as you wish or select from the buttons
      on the ribbon to inser other content

7.   When finished, click Save & Close

Lesson 3.5

Request Access to SharePoint Content

In this book, you have accessed existing content on your
team site. As you collaborate with individuals across your
organization, you may find you need to work with lists or
libraries located on other team sites or with restricted
content on your team site. In this topic, you will request
access to other SharePoint resources.

As a member of a team site, you generally have unrestricted access to all content on your team site. However, certain lists or libraries on your site may be restricted for security purposes, or you may need to work with content that is located on a different team site. When you are denied access to a resource, you don't have to find the correct administrator's email address, identify the resource you want access to, and compose a lengthy explanation why you need access.

You can simply use the request access option on the Open menu, enter information pertaining to the access, and everything is taken care of automatically.

How to Request Access to Content

Request Access to a Resource

To request access to a SharePoint resource:

1. If possible, determine the URL or a detailed description of the resource you need to access so that you can include it in your access request.

2. From the **Open** drop-down menu, choose **Request Access.**

3. On the **Request Access** page, type your request.

4. Click **Send Request.**

Lesson 3 Follow-up

In this lesson, you worked with libraries. SharePoint libraries enable you to store documents, pictures, and other large files in one central location, making them accessible to everyone on your team, and enabling you to control the editing and versioning of files.

1. **What type of documents will you store in your Shared Documents library?**

   Answers will vary, but may include: Pictures and presentations that have to be shared across libraries.

2. **In your environment, what kind of wikis would you use?**

   Answers will vary, but may include: Aa wiki on how to interact with clients, or a wiki on how to use a specific tool to make spell check easier.

Chapter 4

Communicating with Team Members

In this lesson, you will communicate and collaborate with team members.

You will:

- ✓ Participate in a discussion board.
- ✓ Contribute to blogs.
- ✓ Collaborate using the People and groups list.

Introduction

You have collaborated with team members by sharing list items and library files. But there will be instances when you will need to collaborate on ideas and concepts of team members that are not necessarily in document form yet. In this lesson, you will communicate with team members.

Numerous communication tools such as email, instant messaging, and online meetings, are available to collaborate with colleagues in a work environment. However, in order to use these tools, you have to launch several different applications. To capture the information from each application, you have to either copy or paste the information into a new file or save numerous chat conversations or emails. Microsoft SharePoint Foundation now combines all these services into a single location within your team site and captures data without significant human intervention

Lesson 4.1

Discussion Board

In this lesson, you will collaborate with other team members using various SharePoint tools.

One collaboration tool that you might have already used outside the SharePoint environment is a discussion board. In this topic, you will participate in a discussion board.

In many offices around the world, email is the primary method of communicating between individuals. Email is certainly a useful tool, but in order to track conversations you end up saving multiple emails and your inbox quickly reaches capacity. Instead of carrying on a conversation by sending individual emails back and forth, you can discuss a topic, capture a conversation, and save valuable storage space by using a SharePoint discussion board.

Discussion Boards

Definition: A *discussion board* is a method of communication that allows individuals to view and reply to messages as well as post new messages in an online forum. Message boards are generally organized into topics and each topic can contain multiple replies. Discussion boards are often moderated by an administrator who monitors message content and may also approve or reject messages before they are posted.

Team Discussion Boards

A **Team Discussion** board is created by default when a new team site is created.

The View Properties Option

You can view the properties of the discussion by using the **View Properties** option. It displays the subject and the body text of the discussion.

Bulletin Boards and Newsgroups

Before the use of discussion boards and blogs, users shared ideas on a variety of topics via a bulletin board system. This bulletin board used dial-up connections and special software which ran over Usenet, a pre-cursor to the Internet. Bulletin boards and Usenet newsgroups were most popular from around 1980 to the mid-1990s.

Message Threads

Definition: A *message thread* is a series of messages posted in relation to a single topic. The thread begins with an original message and contains any replies to that message. Most message threads can be sorted in chronological or reverse chronological order. A message thread allows you to follow an entire online conversation as it progresses and appears most often in email systems, discussion boards, and newsgroups.

How to Create a Discussion Board

Create a Discussion

To create a discussion:

1. On the **Quick Launch** bar, click the **Team Discussion** link.
2. On the **Team Discussion - Subject** page, click the **Add new discussion** link.
3. In the Team Discussion - New Item dialog box, in the **Subject** text box, enter the subject.
4. If necessary, type the body text.
5. Click **Save.**

Add a Reply

To add a reply:

1. Click the discussion link for which you need to reply.
2. On the discussion page, click **Reply.**
3. In the **Body** text, type the reply.
4. Click **Save.**

Edit a Discussion

To edit a discussion:

1. On the **Quick Launch** bar, click the **Team Discussion** link.

2. From the list of discussions, select the discussion that you need to modify..

3. On the **Items** tab, click **Edit Item.**

4. On the **Edit Item** page, make the necessary changes.

5. Click **Save.**

How to Deleting an Item

Send Alerts on a Modified Discussion

You can delete an item by selecting the **Delete Item** option on the **Items** tab.

To send an alert on a modified discussion:

1. On the **Team Discussion: Subject** page, from the discussion item's drop-down menu, select **Alert Me.**

2. On the **Team Discussion: <Discussion item> - New Alert** page, in the **Alert**

3. **Title** text box, enter a title.

4. In the **Delivery Method** section, select the type of delivery method for the alert.

5. In the **Change Type** section, from the **Only send me alerts when:** section, select an option to indicate the type of change that you need to be alerted to.

6. .In the **Send Alerts For These Changes** section, select an option to restrict the type of alert only for a particular view.

7. In the **When to Send Alerts** section, select the desired option.

8. Click **OK.**

Lesson 4.2

Contribute to Blogs

You and other team members participated in a discussion board. Blogs constitute another communication mechanism provided by SharePoint that enables individuals and teams to share ideas with a larger audience as well as to host discussions. In this topic, you will contribute to a blog.

E-mail, discussion boards, and instant messages are usually conversations between a limited numbers of people. You may have ideas and information that you want to share with individuals other than just team members or even outside your organization. SharePoint blogs allow you to post your ideas and provide a forum for readers to record their comments.

.

Blogs

Definition: A *blog* is an online journal where a blog owner posts topics that can be read and commented on by anyone with access to the site. Blogs were originally a sort of online diary format containing individuals' personal views posted in reverse chronological order on the Internet.

However, they have now evolved into important web-based sources of technical information, news, and expert opinion on a variety of topics. By default, SharePoint blogs are configured to obtain content approval from a reviewer or administrator before a post is published. They are updated on a regular basis and can be maintained by an individual or a group of users. Blog posts contain a title, content, published date and time, and a category

Discussion Boards Vs. Blogs

While both blogs and discussion boards can be used for team communication, each of them have a slightly different focus. A threaded discussion board is a community resource that is intended to capture posting and responses on topics that various contributors can add. Blogs in their original form were intended as a forum for blog owners, either individuals or teams, to post web content on the Internet and share views and opinions in a free-form way, without the need for sophisticated web design or editing skills. As blogs typically include areas for readers to respond to the blog topic, they can also act as discussion boards. However in standard Internet blogs, only a blog owner would post main topics.

The Links Section

The **Links** section on the home page of the team site blog contains two links, the **Photos** link and the **Add new link.** Clicking the **Photos** link, will enable you to navigate through the various steps involved in uploading a photo to the picture library.

On the other hand, the **Add new link** link will enable you to add a new link, which will provide a shortcut to the required webpage.

The Manage posts Option

The **Manage posts** option in SharePoint is a blog tool that enables you to customize the various post lists available on the blog team site. A single click of this option enables you to view the list of blogs posted by other users on the team site. Using the **Edit** button, you can modify the content present in the blog. The **Approval Status** option indicates whether the created blog has been approved or not.

Customizing the Posts Lists View

You can customize the view of the posts lists by changing its view. You can choose one of the options from the **All Posts** drop-down menu to change the view of the posts list.

The Manage comments Link

The **Manage comments** link enables you to make changes to the comments entered for the blog. You can customize the comments added to your blogs by choosing the **Manage comments** option available in the **Blog Tools** section.

The Archives Option

The **Archives** option in SharePoint blogs archives blog posts for future requirements. Based on the month that the blogs are created, they are archived and can be accessed later, by the blog owner or by other users. Each archived blog has a set of blog tools associated with it.

How to Contribute to Blogs

Create a Blog Posting

To create a blog posting:

1. On the OGC team site, navigate to **Our Global Blog.**

2. On the **Home - Our Global Blog** page, in the right hand corner, in the **Blog**

3. **Tools** section, click **Create a Post.**

4. In the **Posts New - Item** dialog box, in the **Title** text box, enter a title.

5. If necessary, in the **Body** text box, enter a body text.

6. If necessary, click **Add** to categorize the blog.

7. In the **Published** text box, click the date picker icon to enter a published date for the blog.

8. Click **Save as Draft** to save a draft copy of the blog.

The **Approval Status** of a blog will remain pending until the site owner approves it. Only then, the blog can be published on the site. A blog can be published by a user only if the user has the site owner rights.

Add a Comment to a Blog Posting

To add a comment to a blog posting:

1. On the **Home — Our Global Blog** page, in the **Blog Tools** section, click the

2. **Manage Posts** link.

3. From the blog lists, click the blog for which you need to add comments.

4. On the **<Blog name> — Our Global Blog** page, add the desired comment.

5. In the **Title** text box, enter a title for your comment.
6. In the **Body** text box, enter the text of your comment.

7. Click **Submit Comment.**

Edit a Blog Comment

To edit a blog comment:

1. On the **Home — Our Global Blog** page, click **Manage comments.**

2. On the blog lists page, click the **Edit** button next to the blog that you need to edit.

3. On the **Comments – All Comments** page, make the necessary changes to the text based on your requirement.

4. Click **Save.**

Edit a Blog Category

To edit a blog category:

1. On the **Our Global Blog** page, on the **Quick Launch** bar, click the Categories link.

2. On the **Categories – All Categories** page, click the **Edit** button next to the category that you need to edit.

3. On the **Categories – <Category name>** page, make the necessary changes to the title.

4. Click **Save.**

Lesson 4.3

Collaborate via the People and Groups List

You communicated with other team members via discussion boards and blogs. There may be instances when you need to communicate directly with specific team members. In this topic, you will collaborate via the **People and groups** list.

When you need to communicate with team members, you could open an email application, enter the email address, assuming you know the individual's email address, and send the message.

But what happens when you don't know the email address of a team member or you need to send an email to all the team members at once? Rather than hunting down email addresses and using a separate application to send your message, you can simply use the **People and groups** list on your team site to view the names of all the team members and communicate directly within the SharePoint team site.

The People and Groups List

The SharePoint **People and Groups** list contains the names of all individuals who have access to a site. By default, the list opens to the site's members group. Within this group, each team member is listed by **Name,** and additional fields display any optional information included in the member's profile. Depending upon the communication services available in the SharePoint network, team members can send email, place Internet phone calls, or send instant messages to other team members directly from this page.

How People and groups List

E-mail a Team Member via the People and groups List

To email a team member via the People and groups list:

1. On the ribbon, choose **Site Actions**, **Site Settings.**

2. On the **Site Settings** page, in the **Users and Permissions** section, click **People and groups.**

3. On the **People and Groups** page, select a user.

4. From the **Actions** drop-down menu, select **E-mail Users.**

5. On the Untitled - Message (HTML) window, in the **Subject** text box, enter a subject.

6. In the **Body** text box, enter the text.

7.   Click **Send.**

Add a new user via the People and groups List

To add a new user via the **People and groups** list:

1.   On the Team Site home page, choose **Site Actions**, **Site Settings**.

2.   On the **Site Settings** page, in the **Users and Permissions** section, click **People and groups.**

3.   On the **People and Groups** page, from the **New** drop-down menu, select **Add Users.**

4.   On the **Grant Permissions** page, under the **Select Users** section, in the **Users**

5.   **Groups** text box, click the directory icon to search for a user to be entered.

6.   In the **Send E-mail** section, observe that the **Send welcome e-mail to the new users** is selected by default.

7.   In the **Subject** text box, observe the default subject that has been entered.

8.   In the **Personal Message** text box, enter the text.

9.   Click **OK.**

Lesson 4 Follow-up

In this lesson, you collaborated with team members using tools such as discussion boards, blogs, and the **People and groups** list. By using the communication tools within SharePoint, you can collaborate with anyone who has access to a SharePoint site and capture feedback directly to your team site without opening other applications or files.

1. **Which will your team use more for collaboration, a discussion board or a blog? Why?**

Answers will vary, but may include: Discussion boards are more optimized for conversation among peers. If there is one content expert, a blog would be used more often than a discussion board because blogs will enable an individual to post ideas and views that would be shared among team members quite often, providing the best information to all members in the team. Discussion boards are more optimized for conversations among peers.

2. **Will you and your team members use the** *People and Groups* **list to communicate? Why?**

Answers will vary, but may include: Yes, the People and Groups list will be used by the team members for communication among team members because it contains information about the team members' profile and thereby enables efficient communication among team members.

Chapter 5

Working Remotely with SharePoint Content

In this lesson, you will work remotely with SharePoint content.

You will:

- ✓ Access SharePoint content from mobile devices.
- ✓ Work with SharePoint content offline in Microsoft Office 2010 applications.
- ✓ Work offline with shared calendars.

Introduction

So far, you have worked with content in a SharePoint team site while your computer has been connected to the network. You may not always be in the office or connected to a network but you may still need access to information on the site. In this lesson, you will work remotely with SharePoint content.

Many people travel on a regular basis and do not have access to the company network. Important information can be saved on your laptop. However, you would have to transfer information to the SharePoint site once you are back in office. In some cases, you might want to work with a smaller device rather than carrying your laptop to remote locations. SharePoint provides several methods for you to access information in lists and libraries whether you carry a laptop or a PDA, and no access to the Internet is required.

Lesson 5.1

Access SharePoint Content from Mobile Devices

Until now, you have been accessing SharePoint lists and libraries from an office computer connected directly to a network. However, you can also connect to the network when you are not in the office and access the same sites, lists, and libraries from mobile devices. In this topic, you will view SharePoint content from a mobile device.

Most of the time, you will probably access your team site while working on your PC or laptop. However, you may be traveling to a customer site or staying in a hotel, and you prefer the convenience of working with a smaller device such as mobile devices rather than carrying your laptop. You can also connect to the network when you are not in the office and access the same sites, lists, and libraries from mobile devices. Your ability to access SharePoint content from your mobile device will help make all these aspects of your job easier.

Mobile Access

By using a Smart Phone, Pocket PC, or web-enabled cell phone, you can access SharePoint sites. A SharePoint site is displayed in a text-only format with links to lists, document libraries, and picture libraries. Once you access the home page of a site, you can navigate to the desired content by clicking text links. Through mobile access, you can work with announcements, task lists, and calendars, open and edit library files, read and author blogs and wikis, and also send emails to contacts directly from a SharePoint site. It is also possible for users to subscribe to receive alerts through text messages whenever changes are made to a particular library, list, or item. This enables users to react instantly to any critical alert generated.

Mobile Access URLs

A *mobile URL* is a SharePoint web address that allows mobile devices to display SharePoint site content. Any site can be accessed from a mobile device by entering the standard URL address and replacing *default.aspx* with *m* in the address

Mobile Access to Lists

You can access a SharePoint list or library from a mobile device if you know the URL pertaining to the SharePoint list or library. However, library and especially list URLs contain coding that make the address difficult to remember. It is much easier to access the site's home page first and then click links to the list or library you want to access.

Default Mobile Views

Almost every list and library has at least one default view that is enabled for mobile access.
Additional Mobile Views

If a list or library does not have a default view enabled for mobile access, the site owner can enable one or more standard views for mobile access. However, not all lists and libraries will have the option to enable a view for mobile access.

Mobile View Limits

Within a mobile view, specific items have character or option limits. For example, there are character limitations on the lengths of titles or of items in lists. There are also limits on the length and number of options that can be displayed in a list or in a choice field. If the text is too large to be displayed in the space available, an ellipsis (...) is displayed in place of the missing content.

Per-Item Limits for Mobile Views

The following table shows you the specific limits for different items in mobile views.

Item	Limit
Web title of a list or library	20 characters
List or library name	20 characters
List item title	20 characters
Column name	20 characters
Single-line or multiple-line text field 256 characters	20 characters
Options in a choice field	10 options
Choices in a choice field	10 characters
Options in a lookup list	20 options
Lookup field item	20 characters
Hyperlink or picture field	20 characters
Attachment file name	20 characters
Displayed attachments for list items	3
Calculated field	20 characters

How to Access SharePoint Content from Mobile Devices

Access the Mobile View of the Team Site

To access the mobile view of the team site:

1. On the team site home page, in the address bar, select **SitePages/Home.aspx** from the URL **http://wss/global/SitePages/Home.aspx** and type **m** to display the URL as **http://wss/global/m**.

The site owner has to configure mobile views for libraries.

2. Press Enter.

3. Observe the mobile view of the team site home page.

Configure Mobile Views for Libraries

To configure mobile views for libraries:

1. Navigate to the library for which you have to configure views.

2. On the **Library** tab, in the **Manage Views** group, click **Modify View.**

3. On the **Edit View** page, in the **Mobile** section, choose one of the four settings to expand the mobile page:

    ✓   If necessary, click **Enable this view for mobile access** to enable the view for mobile access.

    ✓   If necessary, click **Make this view the default view for mobile access** to set this view as the default view for mobile access.

    ✓   If necessary, click **Number of items to display in list view web part for this view** to set the number of items to be displayed in the list view web part.
    ✓   If necessary, click **Field to display in mobile list simple view** to set the field to display in the mobile list simple view

Lesson 5.2

Work Offline with SharePoint Content in Microsoft Office 2010

In the last topic, you accessed SharePoint content with a mobile device. However, if you don't have a mobile device, you can still access SharePoint content when you are out of the office. In this topic, you will work with SharePoint content offline in Microsoft Office 2010.

While traveling for business or working at a client site, you may have to access documents stored in a SharePoint library, or update list data. If you do not have access to the Internet from your location, SharePoint provides several methods of working offline with content in Microsoft Office 2010. Therefore, you can continue to view and edit data when away from office.

Offline Access

SharePoint provides offline support so that you can access SharePoint content when a network connection is unavailable (like when on an airplane or in areas with spotty network access).

When you are working offline, list and library information is downloaded to your computer hard drive. You can view and edit the downloaded data using Microsoft Office (or similar) applications, depending on the type of data you want to work with. Once you are connected to the network again, some programs, such as Microsoft® Outlook®, automatically upload the changes. In other programs, such as Word 2010, you will be prompted to upload the changes.

Offline Capabilities in Microsoft Office 2010 Applications

Several applications in Microsoft Office 2010 suite are integrated with Microsoft SharePoint Foundation, so you can work offline with SharePoint libraries and lists.

Office 2010	Offline Capabilities
Outlook Libraries	Download a single document or an entire document library. If the library is too large, only the titles are downloaded initially. Files can be viewed in Outlook or edited in their native application.
Lists	View and edit standard lists including: calendars, contacts, tasks, and discussion boards.
Word Libraries	Use document check in and check out to edit files while working offline
Access Lists	Connect a standard or custom SharePoint list to an Access table and manage data, run queries, and create reports.

SharePoint Workspace 2010 is a client application that offers fast, interactive access to document libraries and lists on Microsoft SharePoint Foundation 2010. It is the successor of the popular Microsoft Office Groove 2007. It also provides you with a host of automated synchronization features.

137

How to Work Offline with SharePoint Content in Microsoft Office 2010

Work Offline with Content in Microsoft Outlook 2010

To work offline with SharePoint content in Microsoft Outlook 2010:

1. In your web browser, open the list or library that contains the SharePoint content you need to take offline.
2. On the **<List/Library>** tab, in the **Connect & Export** group, click the **Connect to Outlook** button.
3. If necessary, in the **Microsoft Outlook** dialog box, click **Advanced,** and configure the document library or list, and then click **OK.**
4. Click **Yes** to create a folder in Microsoft Outlook 2010.

   — If you connect a library, a folder with the same name as the library is created in the **SharePoint Lists** section of the mail interface.

   — If you connect a calendar list, a folder is created in the **All Calendar Items** section of the Calendar.

   — If you connect a task list, a folder is created in the **Other Tasks** section of the **Tasks** interface.

   1. Double-click the document to be changed.

   2. Click **Edit Offline** and incorporate the changes you need to make.

   3. Save and close the document.

4. If you are online, or the next time that you are online, in the **Edit Offline** dialog box, click **Update** to change the server copy of the document, or click **Do not update server** to leave the server copy of the document unchanged.

Work Offline with Content in Microsoft Word 2010

To work offline with content in Microsoft Word 2010:

1. In your web browser, open the list or library that contains the content you need to take offline.

2. From the document's drop-down menu, choose **Check Out.**

3. In the **Microsoft Internet Explorer** message box, check **Use my local drafts folder** and click **OK** to save the document to the **SharePoint Drafts** folder on your computer. You can now work offline with the file.

4. Use **Microsoft Word 2010** to open the document and incorporate the changes you need to make.

5. Save and close the document.

6. When you are no longer offline, check in the file so that others can view your changes.

7. **Working with Offline Content in Other Microsoft Office 2010 Applications**

8. Using other Microsoft Office 2010 applications such as **Microsoft PowerPoint 2010** and **Microsoft Access 2010** is similar to using **Microsoft Word 2010.**

Lesson 5.3

Work Offline with Shared Calendars

You used Microsoft applications, including the calendaring features in Microsoft Outlook, to access SharePoint content offline. As an organization, there may be a need to go one step further with calendaring, and enable shared calendars to facilitate collaboration and planning among the team. In this topic, you will facilitate collaboration and planning among the team.

There may be times when team members are traveling to a client's place and need to work on calendar list data with no network connection to your server. You can set various options that will enable a team member to work offline with calendar list data. Team members working offline using shared calendars will be able to increase their productivity and meet deadlines.

Shared Calendars

Shared calendars enable users to share information throughout an organization about events in a calendar. Outlook users can share their calendar events with other users and update the shared calendars in a Microsoft SharePoint Foundation team site. An event assigned to a user will automatically appear on the user's calendar. One can view multiple calendars simultaneously to schedule events, thereby preventing conflicts between events.

How to Work Offline with Shared Calendars

Access a SharePoint Calendar Offline and Enable Sharing

To access a SharePoint calendar offline and enable sharing:

1. Access the calendar list in Microsoft SharePoint Foundation.

2. On the **Library** tab, in the **Connect and Export** group, click the **Connect to Outlook** button.

3. If necessary, in the **Microsoft Office Outlook** message box, click **Yes**.

4. In the **Other Calendars** section, right-click the calendar and choose **Open in New Window**.

5. On the **<Site name> - Calendar** window, on the **Home** tab, in the **Share** group, click **E-Mail Calendar.**

6. In the **Send a Calendar via E-Mail** dialog box, click **OK**.

7. On the **<Site name> - Calendar Calendar — Message (HTML)** window, in the **To** text box, enter the email ids

of users with whom you would like to share the calendar.

8. If necessary, in the **Cc** text box, enter the email ids of users to whom you would like to send a cc of the email..

9. If necessary, in the **Subject** text box, specify the desired subject.

10. In the **Body** text box, enter the desired message.

11. Click **Send.**

Add SharePoint Calendar Events from Outlook

To add SharePoint calendar events from Outlook:

1. In the **Outlook** application, access the desired SharePoint calendar.

2. On the **Home** tab, in the **New** group, click **New Appointment.**

3. On the **Untitled - Appointment** window, enter the desired information about the event.

4. In the **Subject** text box, type the desired subject.

5. In the **Location** text box, type the location of the event.
6. If necessary, check **All day event.**

7. On the **Event** tab, in the **Actions** group, click **Save & Close.**

Lesson 5 Follow-up

In this lesson, you worked remotely with SharePoint content. Being able to view SharePoint content from mobile devices such as phones and PDAs and to edit documents and list items in compatible applications such as Microsoft Office 2010 will enable you to continue contributing to your team site even if you are traveling or working from another location.

1. **How will mobile or offline access help your team collaborate when they are not in the office?**

   Answers will vary, but may include: Users can subscribe to alerts that are sent via text messages when changes are made to a list or item. It is also possible for users to edit items offline when they are not connected.

2. **Which application will be your primary offline editing tool? Why?**

   Answers will vary, but may include: Microsoft Office 2010 application will be the primary offline editing tool because it contains various editing options. Another offline editing tool is Microsoft Outlook which can be used offline for editing Word documents with the mail facility.

Chapter 6

Customizing Your SharePoint Environment

In this lesson, you will customize your SharePoint environment.

You will:

- ✓ Customize personal and regional settings.
- ✓ Personalize the page view with Web Parts.
- ✓ Create an alert.
- ✓ Subscribe to an RSS feed.

Introduction

You have worked with all the components of a SharePoint site. But, as you work with
SharePoint on a regular basis, you will want to customize more than just list or library views.
In this lesson, you will customize your SharePoint environment.

Most of us like to customize our day-to-day activities according to our desires. We change the ring tone on our cell phone, decorate and arrange our office space, and choose our favorite home page for Internet access. All these customizations help us to use the tools more efficiently. SharePoint provides several features that you can customize to suit your environment for efficient navigation and increased productivity.

Lesson 6.1

Customize Personal and Regional Settings

Throughout this book, you have worked in a team site that displays generic information based on default settings. The first element of your SharePoint environment you may want to customize is your name, location, and other information that uniquely identifies you. In this topic, you will customize personal and regional settings.

In SharePoint environment, your user name is displayed on the home page and listed on the **People and Groups** page.

Everyone with access to the site will only see the user name your administrator has assigned to you, and most user names are pretty generic. It is not easy to determine who "jsmith" or "mrivera" might be, and if there are two similar names, it is even more confusing. When you add personal information that identifies you and your location, everyone on the team can be sure they are collaborating with the right person.

The Open Menu

The **Open Menu** allows you to customize various aspects of the SharePoint environment.

Menu Option	Description
My Settings	Includes options to edit your personal information, change regional settings, and configure alerts.
Sign in as Different User	Displays the log on dialog box which will enable you to log on to the same SharePoint site with a different user account.
Sign Out	Signs you out of a SharePoint site completely for occasions when you are accessing a SharePoint site from a public computer.
Personalize this Page	Provides controls for you to customize your view of a SharePoint

My Settings

The **My Settings** menu has options to customize your personal and regional information.

Menu Option Purpose

Edit Item Edits personal information including your name, email address, department, job title, and also adds a picture or description of yourself.

Regional Settings Changes the location, time zone, type of calendar, and work week.

How to Customize Personal and Regional Settings

Customize Personal Settings

To customize personal settings:

1. From the **Open** drop-down menu, choose **My Settings.**

2. On the **Personal Settings** page, click the **Edit Item** link.

3. Revise the fields as needed to include the desired information.

4. Click **Save.**

Customize Regional Settings

To customize regional settings:

1. From the **Open** drop-down menu, choose **My Settings.**
2. On the **Personal Settings** page, click the **My Regional Settings** link.

3. On the **Regional Settings** page, uncheck the **Always follow web settings** check box.

4. Make any changes necessary in the remaining sections.

5. Click **OK.**

Lesson 6.2

Personalize the Page View with Web Parts

You customized personal and regional settings of your SharePoint team site. Further, for better interaction with your team site, you might want to personalize its different content structures.

In this topic, you will personalize the page view using web parts.

Every team site has content organized in a structured format. The appearance of the team site remains the same to every member who visits the site. As long as you do not have to visit the site often, its appearance does not matter. However, there could be other sites that you have to visit more often. You might want to customize such sites in order to obtain information easily without much navigation within the site. SharePoint provides you with tools that will enable you to customize or personalize any page so that you can quickly and easily locate information within a team site.

Web Parts

Definition: A *Web Part* is the basic design element of a SharePoint site. All content on a page, whether a list, an image, or a library, is contained within a Web Part. Each page has default Web Parts that correspond to the default lists and libraries on that page. Web Parts can be moved, added, deleted, and edited directly in the browser window.

All Web Parts are located in a gallery, similar to galleries in Word or Excel. Each site has a gallery of Web Parts

Page Views

A *page view* is a format for displaying content on a page. Each page in a site has one standard view that is visible to anyone with access to the page. This is called the *shared view*. Each member can create their own view, called a *personal view*. A personal view is only visible to the member who created the view.

__Site Visitors__ cannot create personal views.

How to Personalize the Page View

Create a Personalized Page View

To create a personalized page view:

1. Navigate to the page that you want to personalize.
2. From the **Open Menu**, choose **Personalize this Page.**
3. If necessary, add web parts to a zone.

149

4. At the top of the zone, click **Add a Web Part.**
5. Select the Web Part you want to add.
6. Click **Add.**
7. If necessary, move web parts on the page by dragging them to a different location.
8. If necessary, modify web parts.
9. From the drop-down menu near the web part, choose **Edit My Web Part.**
10. Change the settings for the web part as needed.
11. Click **OK.**
12. If necessary, minimize the required web part by choosing **Minimize** from the drop-down menu near the web part.
13. If necessary, hide the required web part.
14. From the drop-down menu near the web part, choose **Edit My Web Part.**
15. Expand **Layout**, check **Hidden** , and click **OK.**
16. If necessary, close the required web part by choosing **Close** from the drop-down menu near the web part.
17. On the Page tab, click **Stop Editing.**

Open a Closed Web Part

To open a closed Web Part:

1. Navigate to the page that contains the closed Web Part.
2. From the **Open Menu**, choose **Personalize this Page.**
3. Click **Add a Web Part.**
4. In the **Categories** section, click **Closed Web Parts.**
5. Select the web part that you want to open and click **Add.**

Lesson 6.3

Create an Alert

You personalized the page view by using web parts. Now, you want to send a notification about the changes made, to other site members. In this topic, you will create an alert.

With possibly hundreds of people making changes to site often in a day, it is nearly impossible to update those changes made to every document and list item. It is simply just too much information to try and monitor on your own. Instead, SharePoint alerts can notify you immediately when changes are made to the specific content you want to track.

Alerts

Definition: An *alert* is an email notification that site content has changed. Alerts are available for any list or library in a SharePoint site. When content is changed, an email message is sent to notify the recipient of the change. Alerts can be customized to notify for all changes or a specific change based on certain criteria. The frequency of the alerts is determined when the alert is created.

How to Create an Alert

Create an Alert From Within the SharePoint Content

To create an alert as you view SharePoint content:

1. On the **Quick Launch** bar, click the **Tasks** link for which you want to create an alert.

2. On the **Tasks - All Tasks** page, create alert for the desired item.

   a. Select the item to create an alert
   b. On the **Items** tab, click **Alert Me.**
   c. Choose the **Set alert on this item** option.
   d. On the **Tasks: <Task item name> – New Alert** page, in the **Alert title** text box, enter a title.
   e. In the **Send Alerts To** section, in the **Users** text box, enter user names or email addresses.
   f. In the **Delivery Method** section, observe that the **Send me alerts by e-mail** option is chosen.
   g. In the **Send Alerts for These Changes** section, under **Send me an alert when:**, observe that the **Anything Changes** option is chosen.
   h. In the **When to Send Alerts** section, observe that the **Send notification immediately** option is chosen.
   i. Click **OK.**

Manage Alerts

To manage alerts:

1. On the **Quick Launch** bar, click the **Tasks** link for which you need to create an alert.

2. On the **Tasks - All Tasks** page, select the item to create an alert.

   a. On the **Items** tab, click **Alert Me.**
   b. Choose **Manage My Alerts** option.
   c. On the **My Alerts on this Site** page, add an alert.
   d. Click the **Add Alert** link.
   e. On the **New Alert** page, from the right pane, choose the list or library option that you need to send alerts on.
   f. Click **Next.**
   g. Enter the details for creating a new alert.
   h. Click **OK.**
   i. On the **My Alerts on this Site** page, delete a selected alert.
   j. Select the necessary alert that needs to be deleted.
   k. Click the **Delete Selected Alert** link.
   l. On the **Message from webpage** message box, click **OK**

Lesson 6.4

Subscribe to an RSS Feed

In the last topic, you created an alert. SharePoint also provides another method to notify you of content changes other than email or mobile alerts. In this topic, you will subscribe to an
RSS feed.

Alerts are useful if you require summary of changes at the end of each day or on a weekly basis. For instant notification, using alerts could overload your Inbox quickly. Instead of waiting for an email to let you know when site content has changed, you can view the update immediately through an RSS feed directly from the SharePoint site.

RSS Feeds

Definition: *Really Simple Syndication (RSS) feeds* are XML file formats that are used to deliver the frequently updated content of a website to any application that has feed reader capabilities. Many websites provide feeds that you can subscribe to, so that you can automatically receive updates whenever the website content is changed. The feed contains a headline and a link to the content; it can also contain a description or summary of the feed, and full or partial text from the content source.

RSS can also stand for 3Rich Site Summary.3 RSS feeds are sometimes referred to as web feeds, XML feeds, or often simply "feeds"

RSS Feed Support in SharePoint

In SharePoint Foundation, every list and library is automatically supplied as an RSS feed. You can view RSS feed data directly or you can display the feed data in Microsoft Outlook. RSS feeds in Outlook are created in a separate folder in the Inbox called RSS Feeds.

How to Subscribe to an RSS Feed

Subscribe to a SharePoint RSS Feed

To subscribe to a SharePoint RSS Feed:

1. Open the list or library for which you need to subscribe to an RSS Feed.
2. Select the item in the list/library items page.
3. On the **List** tab, choose **RSS Feed.**
4. In the **RSS Feed message** window, click **Subscribe to this feed.**
5. In the **Subscribe to this Feed** message window, click **Subscribe.**

View RSS Feeds in Microsoft Outlook 2010

To view RSS feeds in Microsoft Outlook 2010:

1. Open Microsoft Outlook 2010.
2. On the left pane, click **RSS Feeds.**
3. Observe that the **RSS Feeds** folder contains folders for any site to which you have subscribed.
4. Select a folder to view its RSS feeds.
5. Click a feed to view its contents.

Lesson 6 Follow-up

In this lesson, you customized your SharePoint environment. This will provide you with the most efficient navigation of the site content and productivity within site pages.

1. **What elements of your SharePoint environment will you customize and why?**

Answers will vary, but may include: The Title, logo, and content structure of the team site can be customized to project a unique team site home page to the user.

2. **If you create a personal page view, what will you change from the standard shared view? Why?**

    Answers will vary, but may include: You can change the libraries view from the team site home page because you have a view that is convenient to you and also add web parts in your personal view that you may use often

Chapter 7

Creating a Sites &
Team Sites

In this lesson, you will create a team site.

You will:

- ✓ Create a site.
- ✓ Create a list.
- ✓ Create a library.
- ✓ Create a discussion board.
- ✓ Create a survey.

Introduction

As we explain in prior chapters, a site collection is a group of Web sites that have the same owner and share administration settings, including permissions. As we explained before, when you create a site collection, a top-level site is automatically created in the site collection. You can then create one or more subsites below the top-level site.

A site collection must exist within a Web application and you can create custom site collection based on an existing Web application. Additionally you can create a Web application and then create a site collection within that application

Whether you're Web application is for a single project or a single team, you should use a single site collection to avoid the overhead of managing multiple sites. However, complex solutions benefit from multiple site collections because it is easier to organize content and manage permissions for each site collection.

All SharePoint 2010 site templates provide the following categories: collaboration, meetings, and custom. When you create a site collection, you select the template that matches what you want the site to do.

Before you create a site collection, you must ensure that the following prerequisites are available:

- A Web application in which to create the site collection.
- A quota template, if you plan to define values that specify how much data can be stored in a site

collection and the storage size that triggers an e-mail alert to the site collection administrator.

Throughout this book, you have been working on an existing team site that contains all the team's lists, libraries, and other content. With time, as new projects are developed, you may need separate team sites to effectively manage those projects. In this lesson, you will create a team site with all the appropriate site components.

A team site can contain numerous list items and library files, with hundreds of members accessing the site daily. As more and more information is added to the site, the home page can become overloaded and difficult to navigate. Rather than add all the site content to the home page, you can organize teams, content, and members into subsites. When you create subsites to distribute the site content, members will find it easier to navigate and can stay focused on the information that pertains directly to their team.

Lesson 7.1

Create a Site

The first step in creating a functional tool for your team to collaborate is to create the site itself. In this topic, you will create a site.

While the team site provides a central location for everyone on the team to collaborate and share information, it may not be the best place for individual project teams to discuss specific projects or ideas that relate to a few team members. When a smaller group of individuals need a separate space to collaborate, you can create a subsite to support those collaboration efforts without providing access to everyone on the team.

Site Templates

When you create a site, you will select the site template that is appropriate for your site's needs. You can choose the desired site template from the Template Selection section on the New SharePoint Site page.

Template	Used To Create
Blank Site	A completely blank site with no default web parts. It can be customized to suit different requirements.
Blog	A place for a single person or a team to post ideas or thoughts and gather feedback from site visitors.
Team Site	A central location for teams to share content, collaborate, and communicate with other team members
Document Workspace	A special type of site that supports team collaboration related to one specific document or meeting.
Group Work Site	A site that is a groupware solution, which allows teams to create, organize, and share information. It includes a group calendar, circulation, phone-call memo, a document library, and other basic lists
Basic Meeting Workspace	A site for teams to plan, organize, and capture the results of a meeting. Lists for managing agendas ,meeting attendees, and documents

	are provided along with this site.
Blank Meeting Workspace	A blank meeting site that can be customized based on user requirements
Decision Meeting Workspace	A site that allows teams to track status or make decisions at meetings. Lists to create tasks, store documents, and record decisions are provided along with this site.
Social Meeting Workspace	A site for teams to plan social occasions. Lists for tracking attendees, providing directions, and storing pictures are provided within the site.
Multipage Meeting Workspace	A site for teams to plan a meeting and capture the outcome of a meeting. Lists for managing the agenda and meeting attendees are provided within this site. It also provides two blank pages that can be customized

Workspaces

Define: A *workspace* is a SharePoint site that supports team collaboration related to one specific document or meeting. Each workspace has built-in lists and libraries to structure the information for efficient team collaboration. Your team may need to collaborate on a single document, such as a proposed budget, that does not belong in the shared library of the team site until it is approved. Team members may also need a place to keep track of budget meetings and a few related documents. These collaboration needs do not require an entirely new team site but they do need a separate and distinct location for storage and tracking. SharePoint provides several workspaces to gather this information using templates that are pre-configured with the appropriate lists and libraries.

Site Creation Options

There are two ways a new site can be created:

- ✓ A site owner creates a subsite.
- ✓ Team members use Self-Service Site Creation, a feature that allows all site members to create a top-level site.

The **Self-Service Site Creation** option is not enabled by default on a site. This option must be enabled by the site administrator.

The Site Actions Menu

The **Site Actions** menu allows site owners to create and manage all aspects of a site.

Site Actions	Description
Edit Page	Allows you to edit, format, and align the contents of a page.
Sync to SharePoint Workspace	Allows you to synchronize the site and its contents to SharePoint Workspace, which is the new version of Microsoft Groove 2007. SharePoint Workspace enables you to work offline with SharePoint content and then update the changes once network is available.
New Page	Allows you to create a blank page that can be customized based on your Requirements
New Document	Allows you to create a document library

Library	to store and share your documents.
New Site	Allows you to create a site for your team or project. You can choose from a collection of available site templates for meetings or collaboration
More Options	Allows you to create lists, libraries, pages, and sites. These options have templates that are similar to those of **New site.**
View All Site Content	Allows you to view all lists, libraries, and discussion boards of a site
Edit in SharePoint Designer	Allows you to create and customize sites, pages, views, workflows, lists, and libraries in Microsoft SharePoint Designer.
Site Permissions	Allows you to give users access to site.
Site Settings	Provides you with access to all the settings of a site.

.

Managing galleries and performing site administration and site collection administration are the advanced site owner or SharePoint administrator tasks.

How to Create a Site

Create a site using Central Administration

You typically use the Central Administration Web site to create a site collection in a stand-alone deployment.

To create a site collection by using Central Administration

1. Verify that you have the following administrative credentials:

To create a site collection, you must be a member of the Farm Administrators SharePoint group on the computer running the SharePoint Central Administration Web site.

2. On the Central Administration Web site, in the **Application Management** section, click **Create site collections**.

3. On the Create Site Collection page, in the **Web Application** section, if the Web application in which you want to create the site collection is not selected, on the **Web Application** menu click **Change Web Application**, and then click the Web application in which you want to create the site collection.

4. In the **Title and Description** section, type the title and description for the site collection.

5. In the **Web Site Address** section, select the path to use for your URL (for example, a wildcard inclusion path such as /sites/, or the root directory (/).

6. If you select a wildcard inclusion path, you must also type the site name to use in your site's URL.

7. In the **Template Selection** section, in the **Select a template** list, select the template that you want to use for the top-level site in the site collection, or click the Custom tab to create an empty site and apply a template later.

8. In the **Primary Site Collection Administrator** section, type the user name (in the form

DOMAIN\username) for the user who will be the site collection administrator.

9. In the **Secondary Site Collection Administrator** section, type the user name for the secondary administrator of the site collection.

10. Designating a secondary site collection administrator is a best practice to ensure that someone can manage the site collection when a primary site collection administrator is not present.

11. If you are using quotas to manage storage for site collections, in the **Quota Template** section, click a template in the **Select a quota template** list.

12. Click **OK**.

Create a site using Windows PowerShell

You typically use Windows PowerShell to create a site collection when you want to automate the task, which is common in enterprises.

To create a site collection by using Windows PowerShell

1. Verify that you meet the following minimum requirements: **See Add-SPShellAdmin.**
2. On the **Start** menu, click **All Programs**.
3. Click **Microsoft SharePoint 2010 Products**.
4. Click **SharePoint 2010 Management Shell**.
5. From the Windows PowerShell command prompt (that is, PS C:\>), type the following command and press ENTER:

— Get-SPWebTemplate

— $template = Get-SPWebTemplate "STS#0"

— New-SPSite -Url "<URL for the new site collection>" -OwnerAlias "<domain\user>" - Template $template

Create a Subsite

To create a subsite:

1. Navigate to the site to which you want to add a subsite.
2. On the **Quick Launch** bar, click **All Site Content,** and click **Create.**
3. On the **Create** page, in the **Pages and Sites** section, click the **Team Sites** link.
4. On the **New SharePoint Site** page, specify the required details.

   a. In the **Title and Description** section, specify the desired title and description for the site.
   b. In the **Web Site Address** section, provide the URL name.
   c. In the **Template Selection** section, select the desired template.
   d. Specify whether permissions should be inherited from the parent site or unique to this subsite.
   e. Specify navigation and navigation inheritance options.
   f. On the **New SharePoint Site** page, click **Create.**
   g. If necessary, on the **Set Up Groups for this Site** page, configure permissions for
   h. SharePoint groups, and click **OK.**

You will have to configure permissions for SharePoint groups only if you chose to create unique permissions for the new site in the **Permissions** section.

Add a Workspace to a Site or Subsite

To add a workspace to a site or a subsite:

1. Navigate to the site to which you want to add a workspace.
2. On the **Quick Launch** bar, click **All Site Content,** and click **Create.**
3. On the **Create** page, In the **Pages and Sites** section, click the **Sites and Workspaces** link.
4. On the **New SharePoint Site** page, fill in the required details.

   a. In the **Title and Description** section, specify the desired title and description for the site.
   b. In the **Web Site Address** section, provide the URL name.
   c. In the **Template Selection** section, select the desired worksapce template.
   d. Specify whether permissions should be inherited from the parent site or unique to this subsite.
   e. Specify navigation and navigation inheritance options.
   f. Click **Create.**
   g. If necessary, on the **Set Up Groups for this Site** page, configure permissions for SharePoint groups, and click **OK.**

Lesson 7.2

Create a List

Your team site might require specific lists that are suitable to keep track of the information needed. In this topic, you will create unique lists suiting your needs. Your team may need additional lists, or a completely different type of list that is not available on the site by default in order to keep track of important information. In this topic, you will add a list.

Each site template has specific lists that are created when a site is created. These lists are sufficient if your team only needs to keep track of content that happens to be an announcement, calendar entry, or link. However, if, you have issues to track or specific project tasks to monitor, the default list formats are not configured for this type of information. When your team needs a different list type, as the site owner, you can add additional lists to your team site as necessary.

List Configuration Options

When you add a list to a team site, you can choose from any of the standard list types available. You will need to choose a name for the list and an optional description. You can also choose to show or hide the list title on the **Quick Launch** bar.

Meeting Workspace Lists

Meeting workspaces have unique lists that can only be
added to a meeting workspace.
List Type Description

.

List	Description
Agenda	Provides a list of meeting topics, the presenter for each topic, and the time allotted for each.
Decisions	Tracks decisions made and meetings and shows results for attendees and other users
Objectives	Provides objectives list for attendees prior to the meeting
Text Box	Provides a space for custom text such as a quote or team slogan
Things to Bring	Creates a list of items attendees should bring to a meeting.

.

How to Create a List

Create a List

To create a list:

1. On the Team Site page, choose **Site Actions**, **More Options.**
2. On the **Create** page,

 Create 　 Site Workflows

3. In the **Communications** section, click the **Contacts** link.

4. Click **More Options.**

5. In the **Name and Description** section, in the **Name** text box, type *New Contacts*

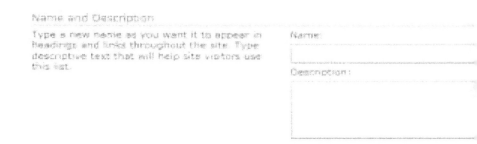

6. In the **Description** text box, type a description.

7. Specify the Navigation

   .

8. Click **Create.**

Lesson 7.3

Create a Library

Earlier in the book you added documents to the Shared Library on a team site. Your team members may not want to store all their documents in a single library. In this topic, you will add a library.

Each team site is provided with a single default library, Shared Documents, when it is created. For smaller teams, this library may meet the document storage needs of the entire team. As the team grows, however, a single document library can become overloaded with thousands of documents and difficult to navigate. To alleviate the problem, you can add specialized libraries and organize documents, pictures, and forms into separate libraries as needed.

Library Configuration Options

Each library has specific configuration options depending on the type of library

Configuration Option	Description
Name & Description	The name of the library that will appear on the **Quick Launch** bar and an optional description of the library.

Navigation	Choose whether the library name should appear on the **Quick Launch** bar of the home page.
Document Version History	Choose whether to track each version of the document.
Document Template	Choose a document template as the default file type for new documents.

The wiki library does not offer an option for version history and neither the wiki library nor the picture library will offer a choice of a document template.

Filter Options

Filters enable you to retrieve and display only relevant information from a library. For example, if you want to view the files modified on a particular date, you can use filters to search and display documents modified on that specified date easily and quickly.

Filter conditions enable you to show all items in a view, or display a subset of items using filters.

Condition	Applied When a Library Item
Is equal to	equals a particular value.
Is not equal to	is not equal to a particular value.
Is greater than	is greater than a particular value
Is less than	is less than a particular value
is greater than or equal to	is greater than or equal to a particular value.
is less than or equal to	is less than or equal to a particular value.
begins with	begins with a particular value

Sort Options

Sorting is the process of arranging the documents present in a library in a specific order. You can sort the documents in a document library in ascending or descending order based on their modification information. Sorting enables you to view and analyze information easily.

How to Create a Library

Create a Document Library

To add a library:

1. Navigate to the site, subsite, or workspace that will contain the new library.
2. **Choose Site Actions, More Options.**
3. On the **Create**

4. in the **Libraries** section, click the **Document Library**

5.   On the **New** page, in the **Name** text box, type NewLibrary and Click **More Options**.

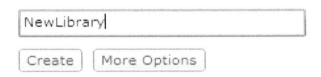

6.   Type a Description in the **Description** text box,.

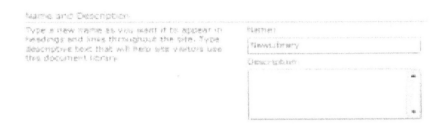

7.   In the **Navigation** section, specify the desired navigation option.

8.   In the **Document Version History** section, specify if each version of documents in the library should be tracked.

9.   In the **Document Template** section, choose **Microsoft Word document** or **Microsoft Word 97 - 2003 document**.

Document Template

Select a document template to determine the default for all new files created in the document library.

Document Template:

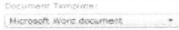

Microsoft Word document

10. Click **Create.**

In a similar way, you can create other libraries such as picture library and wiki library.

Require Checkout for Library Items

To require that library items be checked out for editing:

1. Navigate to the library you want to affect.
2. On the **Library** tab, in the **Settings** group, click **Library Settings.**
3. In the **General Settings** section, click **Versioning settings.**
4. In the **Require Check Out** section, click **Yes.**
5. Click **OK.**

Apply a Filter

To apply a filter:

1. Open the desired library.

2. On the **<Library name>** page, move the mouse pointer over the desired field name and from the drop-down list, select the required field to which filtering is to be applied.
3. From the **<Field name>** drop-down list, select the required item.

To clear the filter, you can select **Clear Filter from <field name>.**

Sort the Documents in a Library

To sort the documents in a library:

1. Open the document library.

2. In the document library, click the *⟨Field name⟩* drop-down list to which sorting is to be done.

3. In the **<Field name>** drop-down list, select the options as required.

   ✓ Click the **Ascending** option to sort the item in ascending order.
   ✓ Click the **Descending** option to sort the item in descending order.

Enable Versioning for a Document Library

To enable versioning for a document library:

1. Open the document library and click the desired document or folder.

2. On the **<Library name>** page, on the **Library** tab, from the **Settings** group, click **Library Settings.**

3. On the **Document Library Settings** page, in the **General Settings** section, click the **Versioning settings** link.

4. In the **Content Approval** section, select **Yes** to enable content approval for submitted items.

5. In the **Document Version History** section, select the desired options to specify if a version needs to be created each time a file is edited in the document library.

6. In the **Draft Item Security** section, select an option to specify the users who will be able to view the drafts in the document library.

7. In the **Require Check Out** section, select the desired option to specify whether users should check out the documents before making changes in the document library.

8. Click **OK.**

View the Version History of a Document in a Document Library

To view the version history of a document:

1. On the **Quick Launch** bar, in the **Documents** section, click the desired document library.

2. From the list of documents in the library, select the desired document.

3. From the drop-down menu of the desired document, select **Version History** to view the version history of the document.

Lesson 7.4

Create a Discussion Board

You have created lists and libraries that help in facilitating better management of your documents to suit your organization's needs. In addition, your organization may want to use a discussion board to facilitate collaboration among team members to record views and ideas on any specific issue. In this topic, you will create a discussion board.

Several collaboration tools enable communication and sharing of critical information within an organization or a department. Discussion forum is an efficient means to facilitate discussions and information sharing. SharePoint Foundation enables you to take this forward and create discussion boards that facilitate recording and saving discussion threads within a SharePoint site.

Trigger Mails

A *trigger mail* is an email that is sent to authorized users whenever an item is posted on a discussion board. A trigger mail is also generated when a user replies to a posting or each time a discussion board item is modified.

Authorized Users

An authorized user is the one who has access to an email account and has permissions to view and post items to a discussion board in SharePoint using Microsoft Outlook.

How to Create a Discussion Board

Create a Discussion Board

To create a discussion board:

1. Display the **New** web page.

    ✓ Display the **New** web page using the **Site Actions** menu.

2. Choose **Site Actions, More Options.**

3. In the **Communications** section, click the **Discussion Board** link.

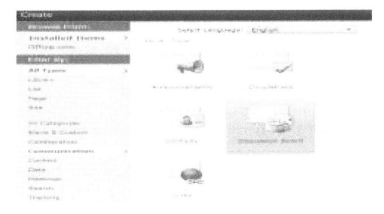

4. On the **Quick Launch** bar, click **All Site Content.**

5. On the **All Site Content** web page, click **Create.**

6. In the **Communications** section, click the **Discussion Board** link.

7. In the **Name and Description** section, in the **Name** text box, type a name for your discussion board.

8. If necessary, in the **Description** text box, type a description of your discussion board.

9. If necessary, in the **Navigation** section, under the **Display this list on the Quick**

10. **Launch** option, select **No** so that the discussion board is not displayed in the **Quick Launch** bar.

11. Click **Create** to create the new discussion board.

Add a New Discussion to a Discussion Board

To add a new discussion to a discussion board:

1. Access the desired discussion board.
2. Click the **Add new discussion** link.
3. In the **Subject** text box, type the subject of your discussion.
4. If necessary, in the **Body** text box, type the body text of your discussion.
5. If necessary, use the options on the **Edit** tab to add character and paragraph formatting to your discussion text.
6. If necessary, attach a file to your announcement.

   a. On the **Edit** tab, click **Attach File.**
   b. In the **Name** text box, enter the file path and name.

✓   Type the file name.

✓   Or, click **Browse** and in the **Choose File to Upload** dialog box, navigate to the desired folder, select the desired file, and click **Open.**

c.   Click **OK** to attach your file.

7.   Click **Save** to create the discussion.

Lesson 7.5

Create a Survey

Throughout the book, you and your team have freely contributed information to lists, libraries, blogs, wikis, and discussion boards. Now you want to gather information from team members based on responses to specific questions. In this topic, you will create a survey.

One thing you can always count on in any organization is that data will need to be summarized and reports generated. Summary data can be an invaluable source of information for managers and survey results can provide valuable feedback on a wide range of subjects. As a site owner, you can create surveys and gather feedback from site users or everyone with access to the team site. When the feedback is summarized in a structured format, it is easy to scan for relevant information.

Survey Configuration Options

A survey has numerous configuration options available.

Option	Description
Name and Description	Specifies the name of the survey that will appear on the **Quick Launch** bar and an optional description.
Navigation	Decides whether to display the survey on the **Quick Launch** bar of the home page.
Survey Options	Specifies options to show the name of survey respondents on the results page and/or to allow respondents to take the survey multiple times
Question and Type	Enters a survey question and the format for the answer. The question types are generally self-explanatory and provide a range of response options, including free-form text and multiple choice.
Additional Question Settings	Chooses additional options based on the type of answer allowed.
Branching Logic	Specifies if an answer to a question will trigger more questions based on the answer

How to Create a Survey

Create a Survey

To create a survey:

1. Login to your SharePoint site as the administrative account.
2. Navigate to the site, subsite, or workspace that will contain the new survey.
3. From the Site Actions, select View All Site Content.

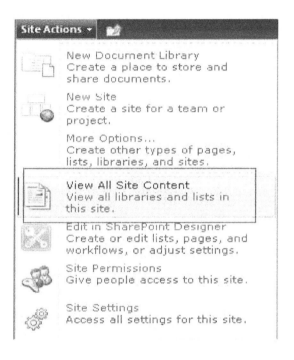

4. Click **Create** page.

5. Click Survey, type in the **NewSurvey**

6. On the right pane, click **More Options**, enter a **Description.**

7. In the **Navigation** section, indicate whether or not the survey should be displayed on the **Quick Launch** bar.

8. In the **Survey Options** section, specify whether to show user names in the survey results and whether to allow users to respond more than once.

9. **Click Create**

10. On the **New Question** page, enter a **Question** and select the **Question Type.**

11. Complete the **Additional Question Settings** section as required.

12. If you need to add more survey questions, click **Next Question;** otherwise, click

13. **Finish.**

14. Complete the **New Question** page as many times as is needed to include all of your survey questions, and then click **Finish.**

15. If necessary, on the **Customize** page, click a survey question to add branching logic to the question.

16. If necessary, click **Change the order of the questions** to reorder the questions.

Respond to a Survey

To respond to a survey:

1. Navigate to the survey that you want to take, click **Respond to this Survey,** and provide your answers.

2. If necessary, click **Save** to save your responses without completing the survey, or click **Next,** and answer the remaining questions.

3. Click **Finish.**

View Survey Responses

To view responses to a survey:

1. Navigate to the survey that contains the responses that you want to view.

2. The **Overview** view is displayed by default. You can display responses in a textbased or graphical format.

3. If necessary, display the text-based response format.

   a. Click **Show all responses,** or from the **View** drop-down menu, choose **All Responses.**

   b. Click a response. You can create, edit, or delete responses, manage permissions, and create alerts from this page.

   c. When you have finished working with the response, click **Close.**

4. If necessary, to display the graphical response format, click **Show a graphical summary of responses,** or from the **View** drop-down menu, choose **Graphical Summary.**

Lesson 7 Follow-up

In this lesson, you created a team site. Rather than adding all site content to a single home page, you can organize the content into subsites. When you distribute the site content over several subsites, members will find it easier to navigate and can stay focused on the information that pertains directly to their team.

1. **When you create a new team site, will you use the default lists and libraries on the site or will you add your own? If so, which lists or libraries will you add?**

   1.

   Answers will vary, but may include: Picture libraries for storing digital pictures that can be used in presentations and Contacts list for storing contact details of colleagues and team members.

2. **In your environment, will you use document and meeting workspaces? If so, what will you use them for?**

   Answers will vary, but may include: Document workspaces for storing documents specific to a particular team event and meeting workspaces to lay down the agenda and objectives for a meeting.

Chapter 8

Performing Basic Site Administration

In this lesson, you will perform basic site administration.

You will:

- ✓ Grant access to a site.
- ✓ Manage site look and feel.

Introduction

In the last lesson, you created a site. Now as the site owner, you need to perform the daily tasks that keep the site running efficiently. In this lesson, you will perform basic site administration.

In almost every organization, network and email administrators perform daily tasks to keep the system accessible to the appropriate individuals and available whenever the resources are needed. As a SharePoint site owner, you will be responsible for performing similar tasks to ensure the availability of site content and provide site visitors and site members access to the resources they need.

Lesson 8.1

Manage Users and Groups

In the previous lesson, you have created a site and added the appropriate lists, libraries, and views necessary for your team. Now you need to make the site available to team members and visitors. As new individuals join the team and others leave, you will also need to modify access to your site accordingly. In this topic, you will grant access to a SharePoint site and manage users and group.

You created a SharePoint site. A host of new users have joined the site. By granting access to team members, your site will become more robust as team members add content and collaborate with each other. Over time, the level of access each group possess may need to change, or you may need to create an entirely new group with specific access rights. As the site owner, you can create, modify, and delete groups as necessary to ensure team members and visitors have the appropriate access to your site.

Site Access Permissions

As a site owner, you can grant access to a site through one of the three default SharePoint groups, or you can add the user to the SharePoint site directly and assign individual permissions based on the user's role.

Permission	Description
Full control	Permits unlimited control of an entire site, including content and access control.
Limited Access	Permits access to shared resources in a site and also items within a site. Designed to grant users unique categorical access to a specific list, library, item, or document, without giving users access to the entire site.
Design	Enables users to view, add, update, delete, approve, and also customize site content.
Contribute	Enables users to only view, add, update, and delete site content.
Read	Limits users to viewing only the content

User and Group Management Tasks

Common SharePoint user and group management tasks that you will need to perform as a site owner include:

- ✓ Creating groups
- ✓ Changing group memberships
- ✓ Modifying a group's settings
- ✓ Deleting groups
- ✓ Deciding the groups that should appear on the **People and Groups Quick Launch.**

How to Manage Users and Groups

Grant Access to a Site

To grant access to a site:

1. Navigate to the desired site and choose **Site Actions☐Site Settings.**
2. In the **Users and Permissions** section, click **People and groups.**
3. On the **People and Groups: <sitename> Members** page, click **New.**
4. In the **Add Users** section, either type the user names, or use the **Browse** button to select the names from the directory.
5. In the **Give Permissions** section, select either **Add users to a SharePoint group** or **Give users permission directly.**

   - ✓ If you select **Add users to a SharePoint group,** provide the name of the SharePoint group.

✓ If you select **Give users permission directly,** select the permissions that the users should be assigned.

6. In the **Send Email** section, check or uncheck the **Send welcome e-mail to the new users** check box. If you want to include a personal message, type the message in the **Personal Message** text box.

7. Click **OK.**

Grant Access to a List

To grant access to a list:

1. Open the list that you want to affect.
2. On the **<List>** tab, in the **Settings** group, click **List Settings.**

3. On the **List Settings** page, in the **Permissions and Management** column, click **Permissions for this list.**

4. Modify the permission level of an existing user's or group's permissions. And Select a user or group.

   a. On the **Edit** tab, in the **Modify** group, click **Edit User Permissions.**
   b. In the **Edit Permissions** dialog box, choose the desired permission level and click **OK.**
   c. Prevent a user or a group from accessing the site.
   d. Select a user or group.

e. On the **Edit** tab, in the **Modify** group, click **Remove User Permissions.**

f. In the **Message from webpage** message box, click **OK** to confirm preventing the user/group from accessing the site.

5. To add permissions for another user or group, on the **Edit** tab, in the **Grant** group, click **Grant Permissions,** add the user or users, configure the permissions, provide a personal email message, and click **OK.**

Granting Access to Libraries and Other Site Content

Granting access to libraries and other site content is similar to granting access to a list, but some of the menu choices will be slightly different.

Create a SharePoint Group for a Site

To create a SharePoint group for a site:

1. Choose **Site Actions□Site Settings.**
2. In the **Users and Permissions** section, click **People and groups.**
3. On the Quick Launch bar, click **Groups.**
4. On the **People and Groups** page, choose **New□New Group** to add a new group.
5. On the **Create Group** page, in the **Name and About Me Description** section, in the **Name** text box, enter a name for the group.
6. If necessary, in the **About Me** text box, enter a description for the SharePoint group.

7. In the **Owner** section, in the Group Owner text box, specify the user or group responsible for the new group.
8. If necessary, in the **Group Settings** section:
9. Select an option to view the membership for this group.
10. Select an option to edit membership for this group.
11. If necessary, in the **Membership Requests** section:
12. Select an option to allow members to join or leave this group.
13. Select an option to accept members for this group automatically.
14. In the **Give Group Permission to this Site** section, choose the desired permission level.
15. Click **Create.**

Adjust a SharePoint Group's Membership

To adjust a SharePoint Group's Membership:

1. Choose **Site Actions, Site Settings.**
2. In the **Users and Permissions** section, click **People and groups.**
3. On the **Quick Launch** bar, click **Groups.**
4. In the **Group** column, click the group that you want to modify.
5. Add users to the group.

    a. Choose **New☐Add Users.**
    b. Browse for and select, or type the names of users to be added to the group.
    c. If necessary, type an email message for the new user.
    d. Click **OK.**

6. Remove users from the group.

a. Check the check boxes next to the users to be removed from the group.
b. Choose **Actions**, **Remove Users from Group.**
c. In the **Message from webpage** message box, click **OK.**

Change a SharePoint Group's Settings

To change a SharePoint group's settings:

1. Choose **Site Actions, Site Settings.**
2. In the **Users and Permissions** section, click **People and groups.**
3. On the **Quick Launch** bar, click **Groups** to view all the groups.
4. In the **Group** column, click the edit button next to the group that you want to modify.
5. On the **Change Group Settings** page, adjust the settings as necessary:

   a. If necessary, in the **Name and About Me** Section, in the **Name** text box, or, **Description** text box, replace the existing text with a new name or description.
   b. If necessary, in the **Owner** section, in the **Group Owner** text box, change the group owner.
   c. If necessary, in the **Group Settings** section, change the group settings.
   d. If necessary, in the **Membership Requests** section, select new options.

6. To delete a setting:

7. Click **Delete.**

8. On the message window, click **OK.**
9. Click **OK.**

Edit the Groups Quick Launch List

To edit the groups in the Quick Launch list:

1. On the **Team site** home page, choose **Site Actions□Site Settings.**
2. In the **Users and Permissions** section, click **People and groups.**
3. On the **Quick Launch** bar, click **Groups** to view all the groups.
4. Choose **Settings□Edit Group Quick Launch.**
5. Modify the **Groups** section to include the SharePoint groups that should be displayed.
6. Click **OK.**

Lesson 8.2

Manage Site Look and Feel

In a previous topic, you customized your own SharePoint environment. As the site owner, you now want to make global customization for the entire site. In this topic, you will manage the look and feel of the team site.

All sites and workspaces are created from the same templates and look exactly the same, with the exception of the title and web address. If nothing ever changed on the site except the content, it would be difficult to quickly see the difference from site to site. By changing the graphics, colors,

197

and layout of a site, you make it unique and easily distinguishable from other sites.

Site Graphics

There are two primary graphics that can be modified by a site owner on a team site.

Graphic	Description
Site Icon	Located in the upper left corner, next to the site title. The site icon appears on each page in the site.
Site Image	It is an image web part. It is located in the upper right corner of the home page by default but like other web parts, it can be moved anywhere on the page.

Other graphics that appear on site pages require web design tools to make modifications.

Site Themes

Each page in a SharePoint site is created with the default theme. The theme determines the colors and fonts used throughout the site but does not affect subsites. SharePoint provides several different pre-built themes and the site theme can be changed at any time, as often as needed.

Any pages in a site that have been customized with a web design tool are not affected by changing the site theme.

The Tree View Tool

Definition: *Tree View* is a navigation tool that displays the content of a SharePoint site in a hierarchy rather than a list. A site owner can choose to enable tree view alone or in addition to the **Quick Launch** bar. When tree view is enabled, all site content appears in a format similar to Windows explorer with each site grouped with its own subsites, lists, and libraries. Items in tree view can be expanded or collapsed, depending on the level of detail desired.

Navigation Customizations

The navigation in a SharePoint site can be customized so the names of lists, libraries, and sites appear exactly the way you want.

Tool	Options
Quick Launch	Add, delete, and reorder list, library, and site names as well as headings on the Quick launch.
Top Link bar	Add, delete, and reorder site names that appear in the top link bar.
Tree view	Enable hierarchical view (similar windows explorer) to use addition to the Quick Launch bar or as a replacement for the Quick Launch bar.

How to Manage Site Look and Feel

Change a Site's Title, Description, or Icon

To change a site's title, description, or icon:

1. Navigate to the site that you want to customize.
2. Choose **Site Actions☐Site Settings.**
3. In the **Look and Feel** section, click **Title, description, and icon.**
4. On the **Title, Description, and Icon** page, in the **Title and Description** section, in the **Title** text box, replace the text in the **Title** text box to change the title.
5. In the **Description** text box, replace the text to change the site's description.
6. In the **Logo URL and Description** section, in the **URL** text box, enter the link to
7. access the logo image file.
8. In the **Enter a description** text box, enter a short description of the image.
9. Click **OK.**
10. **Change the Site Theme**
11. To change the site theme:

   a. Navigate to the site that you want to affect.
   b. Choose **Site Actions☐Site Settings.**
   c. In **Look and Feel** section, click **Site theme.**
   d. On the **Site Theme** page, select a theme.
   e. Click **Apply.**

Change Site Navigation Tools

To change site navigation tools:

1. Navigate to the site that you want to affect.

2. Choose **Site Actions**□**Site Settings.**
3. If necessary, disable the **Quick Launch** bar.
4. On the **Site Settings** page, in **Look and Feel** section, click **Tree view.**
5. Uncheck the **Enable Quick Launch** check box.
6. Click **OK.**
7. If necessary, enable the **Tree view.**
8. On the **Site Settings** page, in the **Look and Feel** section, click **Tree view.**
9. Check **Enable Tree View.**
10. Click **OK.**

If necessary, under **Look and Feel,** click **Top link bar.**

- ✓ If the site inherits Top Link bar links from its parent site, then click **Stop**
- ✓ **Inheriting Links.**
- ✓ If the site does not inherit Top Link bar links from the parent site, and you want to create new links, click **New Navigation Link,** enter a web address and description, and click **OK.**
- ✓ If the site does not inherit Top Link bar links from the parent site, and you want to use the links from the parent site, click **Use Links from Parent** and in the **Message from webpage** message box, click **OK.**

If necessary, change the **Quick Launch** bar.

1. In the **Look and Feel** section, click **Quick launch.**
2. On the **Quick Launch** page, click the **New Navigation Link** link.
3. On the **New Navigation Link** page, provide the web address, description, and heading, and then click **OK** to add links.

4. To add headings, click **New Heading,** provide the web address and description, and click **OK.**

To rearrange the elements in the **Quick Launch** bar, click **Change Order,** use the drop-down lists to select a new order for the links, and click **OK.**

Manage Shared Web Parts

To manage shared Web Parts:

1. Navigate to the site that you want to modify.

2. Choose **Site Actions**, **Edit Page.**

3. For the shared web part that you want to modify, click the drop-down arrow and select **Edit Web Part.**

4. In the **<Web part title>** tool box, change the settings as necessary and click

5. **Apply** and **OK**.

6. On the **Format Text** tab, click the **Save & Close** button.

Lesson 8 Follow-up

In this lesson, you performed basic site administration tasks to manage users, site layout, and site content. By performing daily administrative tasks in your site, you will ensure team members have the appropriate access to site resources and the site is easy to navigate.

1. **When you add users to your SharePoint site, will you add them to one of the three default groups or will you create a new group? If you create a new group, what rights will you assign that group and why?**

    Answers will vary, but may include: Create a new group and assign read-only rights to users who only need to view the site and limited access to users who may have to edit specific site components.

2. **On your team site, will you modify the appearance of any elements? If so, which elements would you modify and why?**

    Answers will vary, but may include: The team logo to better suit the current team and the site theme to give the site a better look and feel.

Follow-up

In this book, you created and edited content in a Microsoft SharePoint Foundation team site, and then you created and managed your own team site. By implementing and using Microsoft SharePoint Foundation, you can leverage the power and flexibility of one of the most ophisticated software tools for team collaboration available today and create a collaborative environment that promotes team productivity and efficiency.

1. **How will you and your team use a SharePoint site in your organization?**

Answers will vary, but may include: SharePoint team site can be used to store information pertaining to the organization. Depending upon the business needs, you can customize your SharePoint team site environment using the different customization options available in the SharePoint team site.

2. **What features of Microsoft SharePoint Foundation will you use the most? Are there features you will not use?**

Answers will vary. but may include: Content structures such as lists and libraries. Lists and libraries will be used often in the SharePoint team site since the day-to-day information can be stored in these items. Apart from these, you can also use the picture libraries in which you can store images related to the team. You can also use other collaboration features such as blogs and discussion boards.

3. **If you are responsible for managing a site, what site owner tasks will you perform most often?**

Answers will vary, but may include: As a site owner, you will perform the tasks such as changing the site features and the site settings of the team site based on business needs.

What's Next?

Microsoft® SharePoint® Foundation 2010 - Level 1is the first book in a two part series. The next book, Microsoft® SharePoint® Foundation 2010 - Level 2, builds on the Level 1 book and focuses on advanced site owner and introductory SharePoint Administrator functions including content management, customization of site content and layout, permissions and access rights, and site collection management.

www.ingramcontent.com/pod-product-compliance
Lightning Source LLC
Chambersburg PA
CBHW080409060326
40689CB00019B/4188